THE BITE-SIZE GUIDE TO VALUE INVESTING

Unlock The Secrets To Value Investing Success

Whether you you are new to value investing or have read every book on the subject, *The Bite-Size Guide to Value Investing: Insights from Great Investors* is an invaluable synthesis of the essential knowledge of value investing that has made investors like Warren Buffett, Benjamin Graham, and Charlie Munger legendary. This book dives deep into every key topic and practice that is part of successful value investing, providing you with sage perspectives from the world's most renowned value investors and investing researchers.

What sets this book apart is its comprehensive distillation of the essential topics and practices within value investing and then synthesis of well accepted adages, quotes, and reflections by great investors or value investing researchers. Each chapter is dedicated to an essential aspect of value investing—ranging from the rationale for value investing, intrinsic value and margin of safety, dealing with mistakes/failures, dealing with bull markets and recessions, using a value investing checklist, and optimising your portfolio. Learn what to buy, when to buy, when to sell, and what to do in different market cycles.

Whether you're a seasoned investor or just starting out, this book provides the actionable insights and real-world lessons you will want to have at your fingertips for regular revisiting. With clear, practical, and digestable guidance stripped of any wasted words, this book will elevate your value investing practice and become an invaluable permanent part of your library.

Richard Busulwa (PhD, MBA, M.Innov) is a senior lecturer and researcher in the business school at Swinburne University of Technology. He is a multidiciplinary researcher in accounting, security analysis and portfolio management, strategic management, entrepreneurship, and digital technologies. He is a stock picker and index fund / ETF investor, he also invests in early/seed stage firms, property, and established SMEs.

The Bite-Size Guide to Value Investing

Insights From Great Investors

Richard Busulwa, PhD

Franklin Oisin

FO

First published 2024
by Franklin Oisin
Adelaide, South Australia, Australian

Library of Congress Cataloging-in-Publication Data
A catalog record has been requested for this book.

ISBN: 978-1-7637962-0-1 (ebk)
ISBN: 978-1-7637962-1-8 (paperback)

10 9 8 7 6 5 4 3 2 1

CONTENTS

The Bite-Size Guide to Value Investing

Title Page

Copyright

Introduction

PART 1: FUNDAMENTALS OF VALUE INVESTING 1

1.1 Definition of Investing 2

1.2 Definition of value investing 4

1.3 Rationale for value investing 6

1.4 Intrinsic value 8

1.5 Margin of safety 10

1.6 Circle of Competence 12

PART 2: VALUE INVESTING PHILOSOPHIES & STRATEGIES 15

2.1 Having an Investment philosophy (or approach, or policy, or framework, or methodology) 16

2.2 Contrarian investing 18

2.3 Deep value investing 20

2.4 Dividend or Income investing 22

2.5 Event driven investing 24

PART 3: THE WHAT/ WHEN/ WHY/ HOW OF VALUE INVESTING 27

3.1 What to buy 28

3.2 What not to buy 31
3.3 When to buy 33
3.4 How much to buy 35
3.5 Why to buy 37
3.6 When to sell 39
3.7 When to hold 42
PART 4: TYPES OF VALUE INVESTING STOCKS 44
4.1 Cyclical Stocks 45
4.2 Growth Stocks 47
4.3 Blue-Chip Stocks 49
4.4 Dividend Stocks 52
4.5 Value Stocks 54
4.6 Index Funds & ETFs 56
PART 5: CAUTIONARY TALES 58
5.1 Timing the market 59
5.2 Speculation 61
5.3 Costs and Fees 63
5.4 Past stock performance 64
5.5 Leverage and Debt 66
5.6 Understanding Risk 69
5.7 Long term perspective vs Short term perspective 71
5.8 Using Money Managers, Funds or Investment Advisors 74
5.9 Momentum Investing 76
5.10 Market Noise 77
PART 6: VALUE INVESTING PRACTICE 79
6.1 Where to find investment ideas 80
6.2 Doing the research 82
6.3 Quantitative vs Qualitative Analysis of stocks 86

6.4 Stock picking criteria	88
6.5 Using a value investing checklist	91
6.6 Decision Making	93
6.7 Evaluating Company Management Teams	94
6.8 Portfolio Allocation / Portfolio Management	98
6.9 Portfolio Diversification vs focus	101
6.10 Monitoring your portfolio / investments	105
6.11 Outperforming the market	107
PART 7: VALUE INVESTOR CHARACTERISTICS & BEHAVIORS	110
7.1 Temperament or Emotional Fortitude	111
7.2 Patience and discipline	113
7.3 Fear	115
7.4 Greed	117
7.5 Over confidence and Humility	119
7.6 Flexibility and Adaptability	124
7.7 Bias and Self delusion	125
7.8 Worry, stress, self- pity	126
7.9 Self Doubt	127
7.10 Indecision	128
7.11 Avoiding herd mentality	130
7.12 Mistakes, Failures, Big Losses	132
7.12 Dealing with Uncertainty	134
7.13 Rational decision making	136
7.14 Psychology of investing	138
PART 8: MAKING TIME FOR CONTINUOUS LEARNING, THINKING, AND REFLECTION	139
8.1 Making time for thinking and reflection	140
8.2 Investor learning & education	141

PART 9: MARKET FUNCTIONING, MARKET CYCLES AND THE FUTURE 143

9.1 Heeding the lessons of market history 144

9.2 Market Efficiency 147

9.3 Market Anomalies or Mispricing Opportunities 149

9.4 Bull markets / Boom markets / Manias / Bubbles 151

9.5 Bear markets, recessions, panics, corrections, and other market downturns 155

9.5 The future 159

INTRODUCTION

Value Investing And Its Promise

Value investing is one of the most time-tested and successful approaches to building long-term wealth in the stock market. At its core, it is often described as the art and science of identifying and investing in undervalued securities or stocks — i.e companies whose current market prices are below their intrinsic or true worth. The intent is for the investor to benefit when the market eventually realises the true worth of the securities or stocks and the stock price rises to be more in line with intrinsic value.

Value investing was pioneered by Benjamin Graham and David Dodd in the 1920s and popularized by legendary investors like Warren Buffett, Charlie Munger, Seth Klarman and Joel Greenblatt. Its origins can be traced back to the aftermath of the 1929 stock market crash, when Graham, teaching at Columbia Business School, developed a systematic approach to investing that would protect investors from the speculative fervor that had led to the market's collapse. His seminal works, "Security Analysis" (1934) and "The Intelligent Investor" (1949), laid the theoretical foundation for value investing and continue to influence investors to this day.

Despite its proven track record, value investing has experienced periods of both acclaim and skepticism from the broader investment community. During the technology boom of the late 1990s and the recent growth stock rally, value investing faced criticism for appearing outdated in a market driven by momentum and growth. However, time has generally vindicated the approach, as value strategies have outperformed growth strategies over long periods, particularly during market corrections and economic uncertainties.

The key advantages of value investing lie in its fundamental principles. First, it provides a margin of safety—by buying assets below their intrinsic value, investors create a buffer against potential market downturns or company-specific risks that may result in stock declines. Second, value investing enforces disciplined decision-making based on both quantitative and qualitative analysis, rather than decisions based on market sentiment or speculation. Third, it aligns with the fundamental principle that price and value are distinct concepts, enabling investors to profit from market inefficiencies and irrational behavior.

For aspiring investors, value investing offers a compelling framework for several reasons. First, it provides a structured approach to investment analysis, focusing on qualitative analysis as well as measurable metrics like cash flows, assets, and earnings rather than abstract concepts or market trends. Second, it cultivates patience and emotional discipline —essential qualities for long-term investment success. Third, value investing's emphasis on fundamental analysis helps investors develop a deep understanding of businesses and industries, knowledge that helps investors to herd pressure and often proves valuable beyond investing.

Perhaps most importantly, value investing offers a path to sustainable wealth creation that doesn't rely on perfect market timing or catching the next big trend. Instead, it rewards diligent research, rational thinking, and the courage to act against market consensus when opportunities arise. As markets become increasingly volatile and complex, the timeless principles of value investing provide a steady compass for navigating investment decisions.

Learning value investing requires commitment and intellectual curiosity, but the rewards—both financial and intellectual—make it a worthwhile pursuit for anyone serious about building long-term wealth in the stock market. Whether you're a novice investor or a seasoned professional, understanding and applying value investing principles can significantly improve your investment outcomes and help you avoid the common pitfalls that derail many investors' journeys to financial success.

Purpose Of This Book

This book distinct from typical investment books in that I primarily wrote it for myself, as a distillation of the essential value principles and practices to regularly revise and internalise. Rather than adding another layer of interpretation to the wisdom of great investors, this book serves as a carefully curated collection of their direct insights, preserving the authenticity and power of their original thoughts and assertions. But despite its concise format, this work makes no compromises on depth or rigor. Instead, it embraces efficiency by focusing on what truly matters while eliminating unnecessary words. Each chapter has been crafted to serve as a quick yet comprehensive reference on critical value investing topics, making it an invaluable tool for both initial learning and ongoing consultation. Many of the investors' insights have to be revisited many times to truly understand them, with each revisit peeling away a layer of misunderstanding to truly get the point eventually. Whether you're analyzing a potential investment or reflecting on your portfolio decisions, this book provides clear, actionable insights derived from decades of collective investing wisdom.

So this isn't a book to be read once and shelved, but a constant reference book—I suggest buying the Kindle version so you always have ready access. As markets evolve and new opportunities emerge, the foundational insights contained here will continue to serve as a reliable compass for making sound investment decisions.

Research For This Book

The research for this book was undertaken over 2 years. It began with an immersive study of the top 100 investment books and top 100 business books. Originally I built a list of investment books recommended by great investors. Then I asked the Large Language Models (LLMs) for lists of the top 100 investment books and synthesised the to lists to arrive at a final list of the top 100 investment books. I repeated this process for the top 100 business books. These 200 books provided a good foundational basis for developing the book's conceptual framework - i.e the necessary parts and chapters of the book. To ensure robustness and completeness, this framework was subjected to analysis by the 3 leading LLMs, which helped identify five additional crucial topics that might have otherwise been overlooked.

Then, to curate the individual investor insights or quotes to include in each section or chapter, initial highlights for from reading the top 100 investment books were gathered and organised into the book's different topics or chapters. These served as a foundation to build on for each topic. These were then enriched with manually sourced quotations from leading value investors. Using a list of the top 100 value investors, I searched online for their top quotes and curated ones to add to each of the book's parts/ topics/ chapters. I then prompted the top 3 LLMs in parallel for the most important quotes on each topic. After carefully verifying each quote, I triangulated and synthesised the results of each LLM to discard what wasn't adding to what I already had and to keep what added to or improved what I already had.

I note that there is likely to be some bias in the final list of quotes selected/curated for each topic in that they were in each case the ones I found most important and that wanted to keep readily accessible for ongoing revision. A different investor might curate/choose a different final list based on their different readings and their different investment experience. If it helps, in terms of understanding potential bias, my hands on investment experience is in stock picking, residential property investment, and startup investing (as a company co-founding investor and as a lead entrepreneur).

This book may just look like a book of quote, but its magic lies in the extensive effort that has gone into building the conceptual framework around which the quotes are augmented, curating the most important quotes, and organising them in a no-frills and easy to access format. This carefully structured compilation is a labour of love to serve both as an introduction to value investing and a sophisticated reference for experienced practitioners.

PART 1: FUNDAMENTALS OF VALUE INVESTING

1.1 DEFINITION OF INVESTING

“An investment operation is one which, upon thorough analysis, promises safety of principal and a satisfactory return. Operations not meeting these requirements are speculative — Benjamin Graham”

"Investing in stocks is an art, not a science, and people who've been trained to rigidly quantify everything have a big disadvantage." — Peter Lynch

"Investing is the art of predicting the reaction of others." — John Maynard Keynes

"Investing is about capturing the benefits of long-term ownership of a business, not about exploiting mispricing in the short term." — Guy Spier

"Investing is about finding great companies and holding them for the long term." — Bill Ackman

“All investing consists of dealing with the future, and the future is something we can’t know much about.” — Howard Marks

"The individual investor should act consistently as an investor and not as a speculator." — Benjamin Graham

"The distinction between investment and speculation in common stocks has always been a useful one and its disappearance is a cause for concern." — Benjamin Graham

1.2 DEFINITION OF VALUE INVESTING

"Value investing is about uncovering stocks that are undervalued by the market." — Guy Spier

"The basic proposition of value investing is simple: if you buy something for less than it's worth and hold it until more of its value is realized, you make money. — Howard Marks

"Value investing is buying a dollar for 50 cents." — Joel Greenblatt

"Value investing is at its core the marriage of a contrarian streak and a calculator." — Seth Klarman

"Long ago, Ben Graham taught me that 'Price is what you pay; value is what you get.'" — Warren Buffett

“You’re looking for a mispriced gamble. That’s what investing is. And you have to know enough to know whether the gamble is mispriced. That’s value investing.” — Charlie Munger

All intelligent investing is value investing—acquiring more than you are paying for. You must value the business in order to value the stock." — Charlie Munger

"The whole concept of value investing can be reduced to

managing a concentrated portfolio of undervalued stocks." —
Michael Burry

1.3 RATIONALE FOR VALUE INVESTING

"Common stocks properly selected and long-range will prove so attractive that I don't believe that other forms of assets are a more attractive or suitable vehicle." — Philip Fisher

"A lot of mutual fund managers don't know what they own. The odds are the best they have ever been for the individual." — Peter Lynch

"In the short run, the market is a voting machine but in the long run, it is a weighing machine." — Benjamin Graham

"Value investing works over time because it is logical, sensible, and has a long history of delivering superior results." — Seth Klarman

"The secret to investing is to figure out the value of something—and then pay a lot less." — Joel Greenblatt

"Value investing is the only tried and true method that delivers outstanding results over long periods." — Mohnish Pabrai

"The beauty of value investing is that it relies on the fundamental truth that the price you pay matters." — Guy Spier

"Value stocks outperform growth stocks over the long term." —

James O'Shaughnessy

"Value investing works because it takes advantage of human nature set to buy hope and sell fear." — James O'Shaughnessy

1.4 INTRINSIC VALUE

"We consider for each of our investments not only whether a security is undervalued but why it is undervalued. If the reason is that there are uninformed or emotional sellers, we become more comfortable." — Seth Klarman

"I always look for red flags. My major red flag all the time is when long governments yield 600 basis points over the yield on the S&P 500. At that point, stocks have always been overpriced." — Peter Lynch

"In the end, the value of your portfolio is not what somebody tells you is likely to happen over the long run but how much other investors out there are going to be willing to pay you for your assets." — Peter Bernstein

What does it profit a man to foresee that a stock will triple its earnings if he pays 4 times its current earnings, the answer is nothing. — Thomas Phelps

"Price is what you pay; value is what you get." — Warren Buffett

"In the short run, the market is a voting machine, but in the long run, it is a weighing machine." — Benjamin Graham

"Intrinsic value is the present value of all future cash flows expected to be generated by an asset." — Warren Buffett

"The stock market is filled with individuals who know the price of everything, but the value of nothing." — Philip Fisher

"Understand the value of the business you're investing in and the price you're paying for that value." — Howard Marks

"If you understand a business, you have an advantage over most people who don't. You can estimate its intrinsic value better." — Mohnish Pabrai

"Investors must recognize that the best investment opportunities occur when companies are temporarily selling below their intrinsic value." — Seth Klarman

"Intrinsic value is not a precise figure but a range that is based on your assumptions." — Charlie Munger

1.5 MARGIN OF SAFETY

"We look for a margin of safety—a buffer between what we pay and what we think something is worth." — Seth Klarman

The function of the margin of safety is, in essence, that of rendering unnecessary an accurate estimate of the future." — Benjamin Graham

"The most important thing is to buy at a price below intrinsic value to create a margin of safety." — Howard Marks

“There's no asset so good that it can't be overpriced and become a bad investment, and very few assets are so bad they can't be underpriced and be a good investment.” — Howard Marks

“Just because something is cheap does not mean it is not going to go down.” — Warren Buffett

“I always look for red flags. My major red flag all the time is when long governments yield 600 basis points over the yield on the S&P 500. At that point, stocks have always been overpriced.” — Peter Lynch

“One of the biggest mistakes you can make is to think that

overpriced and going down tomorrow are synonymous. Markets that are overpriced often keep going." — Howard Marks

"I didn't get rich by buying stocks at a high price-earnings multiple in the midst of crazy speculative booms, and I'm not going to change." — Charlie Munger

"A correction is a wonderful opportunity to buy your favorite companies at a bargain price." — Peter Lynch

What does it profit a man to foresee that a stock will triple its earnings if he pays 4 times its current earnings, the answer is nothing — Thomas Phelps

They don't have to, but most folks lose money. They commit three common mistakes: They overpay, buy businesses they don't understand and neglect to take a long-term approach. These three fatal errors account for most stock market failure. — Ken Fisher

"The margin of safety is always dependent on the price paid. It will be large at one price, small at some higher price, non-existent at some still higher price." — Benjamin Graham

1.6 CIRCLE OF COMPETENCE

“The single most important thing, if you want to avoid a lot of stupid errors, is knowing where you’re competent and where you aren’t. Knowing the edge of your own competency. And that’s very hard to do because the human mind naturally tries to make you think you’re way smarter than you are.” — Charlie Munger

"Invest within your circle of competence. The size of that circle is not very important; knowing its boundaries, however, is vital." — Warren Buffett

"Know your circle of competence and stick within it. The size of that circle is not very important; knowing its boundaries, however, is vital." — Warren Buffett

“I think a weakness of many people's approach to investment is that they try to be jacks of all trades and masters of none.” — Charlie Munger

"Risk comes from not knowing what you're doing." — Warren Buffett

"The whole concept of a 'circle of competence' is that you don't need to know everything, you just need to know what you're good at." — Charlie Munger

"The most important thing is to know what you don't know." —

Charlie Munger

"If you know nothing, you can't do anything smart." — Charlie Munger

"When you stick to your circle of competence, you improve your odds of success." — Howard Marks

"By sticking to what we know best, we ensure the best chance of creating value." — Peter Lynch

"I never invest in businesses I can't understand." — Warren Buffett

"The size of your investment success is not determined by how much you know, but by how realistic you are about what you know." — Joel Greenblatt

"You don't have to be an expert on every company, or even many. You only have to be able to evaluate companies within your circle of competence." — Warren Buffett

"The game of investing is not about knowing everything; it's about knowing enough within your domain to make informed decisions." — Mohnish Pabrai

"Stick to businesses you understand, because your edge is in your knowledge." — Charlie Munger

"Avoid jumping into a business you don't understand because it's a trend. Trends come and go, but your expertise lasts." —–Peter Lynch

"Investors often make the mistake of thinking they have

to venture outside their circle of competence to get higher returns." — Howard Marks

"Sometimes it's the things you choose not to invest in that keep you ahead." — Howard Marks

"The best investors make fewer but more thoughtful decisions within their circle of competence." — Mohnish Pabrai

"Investors who try to be 'jack of all trades' often become master of none." — Howard Marks

"We look for companies that have simple, understandable business models that fall within our circle of competence." — Warren Buffett

"Investing isn't about jumping into the hottest sector; it's about focusing on areas where you have an informational edge." — Howard Marks

"The essence of a sound investment philosophy is knowing what you know and not being afraid to say 'I don't know.'" — Charlie Munger

PART 2: VALUE INVESTING PHILOSOPHIES & STRATEGIES

2.1 HAVING AN INVESTMENT PHILOSOPHY (OR APPROACH, OR POLICY, OR FRAMEWORK, OR METHODOLOGY)

"To be a great investor, you must have an approach, and you have to stick to it, despite the times when it's not working." — Howard Marks

"The market's very emotional but over time, doing something logical and systematic does work. The market eventually gets it right." — Joel Greenblatt

"When proper temperament joins with proper intellectual framework, then you get rational behavior."— Warren Buffett

"I think a weakness of many people's approach to investment is that they try to be jacks of all trades and masters of none." — Philip Fisher

"I didn't get rich by buying stocks at a high price-earnings multiple in the midst of crazy speculative booms, and I'm not going to change." — Charlie Munger

"Heads I win; tails I don't lose much. That's the kind of investment strategy I can live with." — Mohnish Pabrai

"Having a disciplined sell strategy is just as important as having a disciplined buy strategy." — James O'Shaughnessy

"Avoiding greed and fear is essential in value investing; stick to your framework and be patient." — Mohnish Pabrai

"Heads I win; tails I don't lose much. That's the kind of investment strategy I can live with." — Mohnish Pabrai

"The best way to measure your investing success is not by whether you're beating the market but by whether you've put in place a financial plan and a behavioral discipline that are likely to get you where you want to go." — Benjamin Graham

Some Scandinavian canoeists succeeded in getting through all the rapids of Scandinavia and they thought they would continue their success by tackling all the whirlpools in North America - the death rate was 100%. A big whirlpool is something you want to avoid. So is an intense ideology; particularly when your companions are all true believers. — Charlie Munger

"I don't look to jump over 7-foot bars; I look around for 1-foot bars that I can step over." — Warren Buffett

2.2 CONTRARIAN INVESTING

“The tour we've taken through the last century proves that market irrationality of an extreme kind periodically erupts -- and compellingly suggests that investors wanting to do well had better learn how to deal with the next outbreak.” — Warren Buffett

“Being extremely early is tantamount to being wrong, so contrarians are well advised to develop an understanding of the psychology of the sellers.” — Seth Klarman

"Buy when there's blood in the streets, even if the blood is your own." — Baron Rothschild

"Be fearful when others are greedy and greedy when others are fearful." — Warren Buffett

"The time of maximum pessimism is the best time to buy, and the time of maximum optimism is the best time to sell." — Sir John Templeton

"The intelligent investor is a realist who sells to optimists and buys from pessimists." — Benjamin Graham

"It is impossible to produce superior performance unless you do something different from the majority." — Sir John Templeton

"The trick is not to learn to trust your gut feelings, but rather to discipline yourself to ignore them." — Peter Lynch

"You can't buy what is popular and do well." — Warren Buffett

"The best investments are usually the ones nobody wants." — John Neff

"You make most of your money in a bear market; you just don't realize it at the time." — Shelby Cullom Davis

"The contrarian approach is just as much about being anti-momentum as it is about being anti-consensus." — Howard Marks

2.3 DEEP VALUE INVESTING

"Deep value stocks are often found in industries that are out of favor, offering significant upside when the market recognizes their true worth." — David Dreman

"To succeed in deep value investing, one must have the conviction to act when others are fearful." — Sir John Templeton

"Deep value opportunities arise when markets overreact to bad news, pushing stock prices below their intrinsic value." — Michael Price

"Deep value investing is about finding dollars selling for fifty cents." — Walter Schloss

"Patience is essential in deep value investing, as the market may take time to recognize the true value of an asset." — Mohnish Pabrai

"Deep value investors focus on the margin of safety, ensuring that they invest with a significant cushion against loss." — Seth Klarman

"In deep value investing, one must be comfortable being uncomfortable, as the best opportunities are often in distressed or unpopular areas." — Howard Marks

"Deep value investing is not about chasing trends but about

uncovering hidden gems that others have overlooked."— Joel Greenblatt

"Deep value investing requires patience and discipline, as the best opportunities often lie where others are not looking." — Seth Klarman

"Investors must be willing to dig deep to find the true value hidden beneath the surface." — Benjamin Graham

2.4 DIVIDEND OR INCOME INVESTING

"The beauty of dividends is that they provide a return on investment without the need to sell the shares." — Peter Lynch

"Dividends don't lie. A company's willingness and ability to pay steady dividends over time—and its power to increase them—provide a good clue about its fundamentals." — Seth Klarman

"Dividends are a sign of corporate strength and commitment to shareholders." — Warren Buffett

"I would never buy a stock that doesn't pay a dividend." — Kevin O'Leary

"Dividends are the only return on investment that is certain." — David Dreman

"Dividend growth is an important indicator of a company's financial health and future prospects." — Warren Buffett

"High dividend yields can often be a red flag indicating potential problems in a company." — Benjamin Graham

"Dividends are tangible evidence of a company's earnings power and financial stability." — Seth Klarman

"Dividend-paying stocks have historically outperformed non-dividend-paying stocks over the long term." — Jeremy Siegel

"Dividends force management to be disciplined with capital allocation." — Warren Buffett

"Companies that pay dividends attract investors who value stability and income, which can reduce stock price volatility." — Peter Lynch

"The power of compounding dividends over time is one of the most underappreciated aspects of investing." — Warren Buffett

2.5 EVENT DRIVEN INVESTING

"Event-driven investing involves buying and selling securities whose prices are expected to be influenced by a particular upcoming event." — Seth Klarman

"Event-driven investing is about capitalizing on the mispricings that occur before, during, or after a corporate event." —Joel Greenblatt

"In times of market stress, events can create dislocations that offer exceptional investment opportunities." — Howard Marks

"Understanding the potential outcomes of an event is crucial for investors seeking to capitalize on special situations." — David Einhorn

"Market events can create significant volatility, but they also present unique opportunities for disciplined investors." — Howard Marks

"An investment strategy that considers corporate events can uncover value that others might overlook." — Michael Price

"Event-driven strategies require patience and a deep understanding of the factors that can influence the outcome." — John Paulson

"Investors must be prepared for any event that could impact their investments, including those that are unforeseen."

— Warren Buffett

"Event risk is a part of investing, but it can also be a source of significant opportunity."
— Carl Icahn

"By focusing on events that alter a company's fundamentals, investors can identify mispricings in the market."
— Seth Klarman

"Special situations arise when an event creates a disparity between price and value."
— Joel Greenblatt

"The key to event-driven investing is understanding how an event will impact a company's future prospects."
— David Einhorn

"Market reactions to events are often driven by emotion, creating opportunities for rational investors."
— Howard Marks

"Event-driven strategies can yield significant returns when the outcome of an event is misjudged by the market."
— John Paulson

"Investing around events requires a deep dive into the specifics, as no two events are exactly alike."
— Michael Price

"An unexpected event can disrupt markets, but it also can present the chance to buy quality assets at discounted prices."
— Warren Buffett

"The market's initial reaction to an event is often an overreaction, providing opportunities for those who can see beyond the noise."
— Seth Klarman

"Great investment opportunities come around when excellent

companies are surrounded by unusual circumstances that cause the stock to be misappraised."
— Warren Buffett

“The years ahead will occasionally deliver major market declines, even panics, that will affect virtually all stocks. No one can tell you when these traumas will occur. This does not bother Charlie [Munger] and me. Indeed, we enjoy such price declines, if we have funds available to increase our positions. — Warren Buffett

So smile when you read a headline that says ‘Investors lose as market falls.’ Edit it in your mind to ‘Disinvestors lose as market falls—but investors gain.’ Though writers often forget this truism, there is a buyer for every seller and what hurts one necessarily helps the other. — Warren Buffett

“Far more money has been lost by investors preparing for corrections, or trying to anticipate corrections, than has been lost in corrections themselves.” — Peter Lynch

“The market can stay irrational longer than you can stay solvent.” — John Maynard Keynes

“Timing is everything. If you are early or late to an event, you could be missing the opportunity.” — Michael Burry

“You need to have a contrarian view of events to outperform, but you must understand when the crowd has it wrong.” — Bill Ackman

"Event-driven strategies require not just analysis but also an understanding of the probabilities associated with different outcomes."
— David Einhorn

PART 3: THE WHAT/ WHEN/ WHY/ HOW OF VALUE INVESTING

3.1 WHAT TO BUY

“I think I am safe in asserting that the margin trader, speculator, gambler, or whatever you choose to designate the average man who goes to Wall Street after easy money, does not lose money when he sells. He loses it when he buys!” — Edwin Lefevre

“I have a very simple strategy. I buy good companies at attractive prices. Then I sit on them.” — Philip Carret

“Buy only what you understand, believe in, and intend to stick with -- even when others are chasing the next miracle.” — Peter Lynch

“People who chase growth, who chase highfliers, inevitably lose because they paid a premium price. They lose to the people who have more patience and more discipline.”— Seth Klarman

“I never in all my life bought a stock because I liked it. I bought it because it was a cheaper bargain than any similar stock I would buy anywhere in the rest of the world.” —John Templeton

“Just because something is cheap does not mean it is not going to go down.” — Warren Buffett

I am not willing to incur risk of substantial permanent capital loss in seeking better long term performance.” — Warren Buffett

"We look for businesses that have dominant market positions, high barriers to entry, limited cyclicality, high returns on capital, and great management teams." — Bill Ackman

“My experience teaches me that by far the largest losses have been sustained by investors through buying securities of inferior quality under favorable general conditions.” — Benjamin Graham

"Only buy something that you’d be perfectly happy to hold if the market shut down for 10 years." — Warren Buffett

"We're trying to find things that are cheap—where we feel like we understand the value and we're buying at a big discount to that." — Joel Greenblatt

"In business, I look for economic castles protected by unbreachable moats." — Warren Buffett

"We try to buy stocks with low price-to-book ratios." — Walter Schloss

"All you have to do is find undervalued stocks and invest in them." — Michael Burry

"Low P/E stocks outperform high P/E stocks over the long term." — John Neff

"Focus on companies with a strong franchise and barriers to entry." — Bruce Greenwald

"Buy companies with strong histories of profitability and with a dominant business franchise." — Warren Buffett

If you buy right, you buy an unpopular and much depressed stock of a good business. In time the firm’s quality will be recognized by others, and then the stock will become more popular and rise. But no one can tell just when this will happen. —Irving Kahn

3.2 WHAT NOT TO BUY

"My experience teaches me that by far the largest losses have been sustained by investors through buying securities of inferior quality under favorable general conditions." — Benjamin Graham

They don't have to, but most folks lose money. They commit three common mistakes: They overpay, buy businesses they don't understand and neglect to take a long-term approach. These three fatal errors account for most stock market failure. — Ken Fisher

Never invest in a business you cannot understand. —Warren Buffett

After 25 years of buying and supervising a great variety of businesses, Charlie [Munger] and I have not learned how to solve difficult business problems. What we have learned is to avoid them." — Warren Buffett

"A great business at a fair price is superior to a fair business at a great price." — Warren Buffett

If you take a business that is a good business, but not a fabulous business, they tend to fall into two categories. One is the business where the whole reported profit just sits there in surplus cash at the end of the year. And you can take it out of the business and the business will do just as well without it as it would if it stayed in the business. The second business is one that reports the 12 percent on capital but there's never any cash.

It reminds me of the used construction equipment business of my old friend, John Anderson. And he used to say, “In my business, every year you make a profit, and there it is, sitting in the yard.” And there are an awful lot of businesses like that, where just to keep going, to stay in place, there’s never any cash. Now, that business doesn’t enable headquarters to drag out all the cash and invest it elsewhere. We hate that kind of a business — Charlie Munger

"We’re not generally enthused about businesses where we think the future economics will be way less than the current economics." — Charlie Munger

"Avoid companies with commodity-type products that are subject to severe price competition and cyclical downturns." — Philip Fisher

"I avoid cyclical industries because their futures are too unpredictable for me." — Guy Spier

3.3 WHEN TO BUY

“There will be bear markets about twice every 10 years and recessions about twice every 10 or 12 years but nobody has been able to predict them reliably. So the best thing to do is to buy when shares are thoroughly depressed and that means when other people are selling.” — John Templeton

“You want to be greedy when others are fearful. You want to be fearful when others are greedy. It's that simple.”— Warren Buffett

“When people are desperately trying to sell, I buy. When people are desperately trying to buy, I sell. It has worked out very well over the years.” — John Templeton

“The best time to get involved with cyclicals is when the economy is at its weakest, earnings are at their lowest, and public sentiment is at its bleakest.” — Peter Lynch

“A correction is a wonderful opportunity to buy your favorite companies at a bargain price.” — Peter Lynch

"The intelligent investor is a realist who sells to optimists and buys from pessimists." — Benjamin Graham

"The time of maximum pessimism is the best time to buy, and the time of maximum optimism is the best time to sell." — Sir John Templeton

"Invest at the point of maximum pessimism." — Sir John Templeton

"When good opportunities are scarce, I am happy to hold cash. When I find an exceptional opportunity, I invest heavily." — Bruce Berkowitz

"The best time to buy is when assets are shunned and unloved." — James Montier

"We try to buy stocks with low price-to-book ratios during times when the market is pessimistic." — Walter Schloss

"Buy when the herd is panic selling and prices are depressed." — David Dreman

"The most significant gains come when you buy something because everyone else is selling, not when you buy because everyone else is buying." — Howard Marks

"Great investment opportunities come around when excellent companies are surrounded by unusual circumstances that cause the stock to be misappraised." — Warren Buffett

3.4 HOW MUCH TO BUY

“Good investing requires a weird combination of patience and aggression. And not many people have it.”— Charlie Munger

“You want to be greedy when others are fearful. You want to be fearful when others are greedy. It's that simple.” — Warren Buffett

What you have to learn is to fold early when the odds are against you. Or if you have a big edge, back it heavily because you don’t get a big edge often. Opportunity comes, but it doesn’t come often, so seize it when it does come — Charlie Munger

Opportunities come infrequently. When it rains gold, put out the bucket, not the thimble —Warren Buffett

"Our policy is to concentrate holdings. We try to invest significant amounts in a few companies that meet our criteria." — Warren Buffett

"Few bets, big bets, infrequent bets." — Mohnish Pabrai

"When good opportunities are scarce, I am happy to hold cash. When I find an exceptional opportunity, I invest heavily." — Bruce Berkowitz

"It's extremely hard to find ideas that meet our criteria, so when we find one, we make a large commitment." — Lou Simpson

"When good opportunities are scarce, I am happy to hold cash. When I find an exceptional opportunity, I invest heavily." — Bruce Berkowitz

3.5 WHY TO BUY

“The inescapable fact is that the value of an asset, whatever its character, cannot over the long term grow faster than its earnings do.” — Warren Buffett

"Know what you own, and know why you own it." — Peter Lynch

"We have to deal in things that we're capable of understanding, and then, once we're over that filter, we have to have a business with some intrinsic characteristics that give it a durable competitive advantage." — Charlie Munger

"The stock buyer should understand clearly the reasons why he is purchasing a stock and should have sufficient factual data to support his decision." — Philip Fisher

"Heads I win; tails I don't lose much. That's the kind of investment strategy I can live with." — Mohnish Pabrai

"The best investors do not target returns; they focus first on risk." — Seth Klarman

"Investing is about capturing the benefits of long-term ownership of a business, not about exploiting mispricing in the short term." — Guy Spier

"Investors should buy stocks when they are cheap and sell them when they reach their intrinsic value." — Bruce Greenwald

"Successful stocks don't have to be high-tech or fashionable. Look for companies that are selling at bargain prices." — John Neff

"If you know something others don't, or if you think differently, you may find opportunities that others miss." — Bruce Berkowitz

"Investing is about finding great companies and holding them for the long term." — Bill Ackman

3.6 WHEN TO SELL

"If the job has been correctly done when a common stock is purchased, the time to sell it is—almost never." — Philip Fisher

"Selling your winners and holding your losers is like cutting the flowers and watering the weeds." — Peter Lynch

"Our favorite holding period is forever." - Warren Buffett

“When people are desperately trying to sell, I buy. When people are desperately trying to buy, I sell. It has worked out very well over the years.” — John Templeton

"The intelligent investor is a realist who sells to optimists and buys from pessimists." — Benjamin Graham

"We sell when we lose confidence in management or when the company's fundamentals deteriorate." — Lou Simpson

"Having a disciplined sell strategy is just as important as having a disciplined buy strategy." — James O'Shaughnessy

"I try to sell when the market price exceeds my calculated intrinsic value." — Michael Burry

"We sell when the investment reaches our estimate of intrinsic value or when we find a better opportunity." — David Einhorn

"We sell when we believe the future returns from the investment are unlikely to be attractive." — Bill Ackman

"I sell when a stock's price-earnings ratio approaches or exceeds its growth rate." — John Neff

"Sell when the market price exceeds intrinsic value by a margin that compensates for the risk of holding." — Bruce Greenwald

"Sell when the stock becomes overvalued relative to its historical norms." — David Dreman

"The time to sell an asset is when you have found a much better bargain to replace it." — Sir John Templeton

"I sell when I realize I've made a mistake or when the fundamentals deteriorate." — Guy Spier

"Selling is not a matter of emotion but of necessity when the value is fully realized." — Howard Marks

"We sell when the catalyst we expected has played out and the stock has reached our target price." — Joel Greenblatt

"We will sell when we believe we can replace an investment with one that has a more favorable risk/reward profile." — Seth Klarman

"Sell when you find a significantly better bargain, not because of short-term market fluctuations." — Sir John Templeton

"We sell when the investment's risk outweighs its potential reward." — Bruce Berkowitz

"We decide to sell when the company's fundamentals no longer support our investment thesis." — Lou Simpson

"We exit an investment when we believe its future potential no longer justifies the associated risks." — Bill Ackman

"Investors should buy stocks when they are cheap and sell them when they reach their intrinsic value." — Bruce Greenwald

3.7 WHEN TO HOLD

“If a stock has gone sideways for a couple of years, and the fundamentals are decent, and you can find something new that's positive in the company, then if you're wrong, the stock will probably continue to go sideways, and you won't lose a lot of money. But if you're right, that stock is going north.” — Peter Lynch

“One of the oldest sayings on Wall Street is "Let your winners run, and cut your losers." It's easy to make a mistake and do the opposite, pulling out the flowers and watering the weeds.” — Peter Lynch

"If the job has been correctly done when a common stock is purchased, the time to sell it is—almost never." — Philip Fisher

"Selling your winners and holding your losers is like cutting the flowers and watering the weeds." — Peter Lynch

"Our favorite holding period is forever." - Warren Buffett

"Time is the friend of the wonderful company, the enemy of the mediocre." — Warren Buffett

"The true investor scarcely ever is forced to sell his shares, and at all other times he is free to disregard the current price quotation." — Benjamin Graham

"The big money is not in the buying and selling... but in the waiting." — Charlie Munger

PART 4: TYPES OF VALUE INVESTING STOCKS

4.1 CYCLICAL STOCKS

“You can't go to sleep holding cyclical stocks for a decade and expect to be richly rewarded. The rich rewards are in growth stocks and special situations.” — Peter Lynch

“The best time to get involved with cyclicals is when the economy is at its weakest, earnings are at their lowest, and public sentiment is at its bleakest.” — Peter Lynch

“In cyclicals, a period of silly prices is followed by a period of sobriety.” — Peter Lynch

"The investor should be aware that even the best cyclical companies are inherently risky in terms of earnings stability." —Benjamin Graham

"The problem with commodities and cyclical businesses is that you can go years when the price gets very weak and stays weak for a long time." — Warren Buffett

"Cyclical companies may appear cheap at the peak of their cycles and expensive at the troughs. Investors must understand the cycles." — Seth Klarman

"Investors can do well with cyclical stocks if they buy during pessimism and sell during optimism." — John Neff

"I prefer simple businesses with low uncertainty, not cyclical ones where predicting the future is challenging." — Mohnish Pabrai

"Cyclical stocks can be value traps if bought at the wrong point in the cycle." — David Dreman

"It's difficult to time the cycles, so I focus on companies with consistent earnings." — Joel Greenblatt

"The time of maximum pessimism in cyclical industries can offer great opportunities." — Sir John Templeton

"Cyclical stocks require a margin of safety because earnings can disappear quickly." — Michael Burry

"Cyclical stocks can offer value, but only if one is patient and understands the cycle." — James Montier

"We tend to avoid highly cyclical businesses because their earnings are hard to predict." — David Einhorn

"Cyclicals can be dangerous; they look cheap at the top and expensive at the bottom." — Jeremy Grantham

4.2 GROWTH STOCKS

"Maybe you're right 5 or 6 times out of 10. But if your winners go up 4 or 10 or 20 fold, it makes up for the ones where you lost 50%, 75%, or 100%." — Peter Lynch

"Growth stock investing may be more a philosophy of buying what is popular. Value investing is more a philosophy of buying what is out of favor." — Chris Browne

"When picking a list of growth stocks for long-term investment, broad diversification of the risk is the first and most important principle to follow. No one can look ahead five or ten years and say what is the most promising industry or the best stock to own." — T. Rowe Price

""Growth stocks" can be defined as shares in business enterprises which have demonstrated favorable underlying long-term growth in earnings and which, after careful research study, give indications of continued secular growth in the future." — T. Rowe Price

"If you are in the right companies, the potential rise can be so enormous that everything else is secondary." — Philip Fisher

"People who chase growth, who chase highfliers, inevitably lose because they paid a premium price. They lose to the people who have more patience and more discipline." — Seth Klarman

"The successful purchase of growth stocks requires two rather obvious conditions: First, that their prospect of growth be realized; and, second, that the market has not already pretty well discounted these growth prospects." — Benjamin Graham

"To my mind, the so-called growth-stock investor -- or the average security analyst for that matter -- has no idea of how much to pay for a growth stock, how many stocks to buy to obtain the desired return, or how their prices will behave." — Benjamin Graham

"A hot stock, like a hot stove, should be handled with care." — Benjamin Graham

"Many mistakes have been made in buying growth stocks on the theory that the future will duplicate the past." — Benjamin Graham

"If you're lucky enough to have one golden egg in your portfolio, it may not matter if you have a couple of rotten ones in there with it." — Peter Lynch

4.3 BLUE-CHIP STOCKS

"It's far better to buy a wonderful company at a fair price than a fair company at a wonderful price." — Warren Buffett

"You don't have to trade actively to make good returns. Sometimes, holding quality blue chips over long periods is all it takes." — Philip Fisher

"Blue-chip companies often represent quality and stability, but investors should be cautious of paying too much for them." — Benjamin Graham

"Blue-chip companies often provide stability in uncertain times, but don't expect spectacular returns unless you buy them at the right price." — Benjamin Graham

"If a business is worth buying, it will be even better to buy it when it's unpopular. That's how blue chips turn into blue bargains." — John Templeton

"The key to making money in stocks is not to get scared out of them. This is why blue chips are favored; they help investors sleep at night." — Peter Lynch

"A great company keeps performing, but to be a great investment, you must be disciplined about the price you pay—even for a blue-chip." — Seth Klarman

"Even in blue-chip stocks, buying high can be disastrous. Prices and fundamentals both matter." — David Dreman

"The beauty of blue chips is in their reliability, but if you pay too much, they offer little in terms of real value." — Howard Marks

"While blue chips have longevity, the price you pay determines the return you'll get. Even the best businesses are not immune to overvaluation." — Warren Buffett

"The advantage of blue-chip stocks is that they offer a 'sleep-well-at-night' factor, but that's no reason to ignore valuation." — Joel Greenblatt

"Blue-chip companies provide safety, but safety and high returns rarely go together. Valuation is always key." — Mohnish Pabrai

"The top blue-chip stocks have a proven track record, which is why people love them. Just don't expect great returns unless you buy them during downturns." — Charlie Munger

"You buy blue chips for stability, but if you overpay, you might be locking in modest returns. Valuation is still king." — David Einhorn

"Blue-chip stocks give you the comfort of owning something solid. However, comfort is often expensive in the stock market." — Warren Buffett

"Blue chips are safe, but safety often means mediocre returns. To profit, even in blue chips, buy them when they're undervalued." — John Neff

"A blue chip's strong fundamentals make it easier to predict future earnings, but only if the price isn't inflated." — Thomas Rowe Price

4.4 DIVIDEND STOCKS

"If you're looking to own a stock for its dividend, make sure the business itself is sound, or the dividend won't last." — Warren Buffett

"Dividend payments impose a discipline on management because they cannot hoard cash; they have to perform consistently." — John Bogle

"Dividends are tangible proof of profitability. They are a way to generate cash for investors without them having to sell their shares." — John Neff

"Dividends don't lie. They're a clear indication of a company's profitability and commitment to returning value to shareholders." — Geraldine Weiss

"The beauty of dividends is that they provide a steady stream of cash flow, even if the stock market is volatile." — Joel Greenblatt

"Investing in dividend-paying stocks can serve as a hedge in volatile markets, providing income while you wait for the market to recover." — Seth Klarman

"It's more important to increase your capital in the long run than to receive dividends in the short run." — Peter Lynch

"Dividend growth stocks give you the benefit of compounding

income, which can result in significant long-term gains." — Warren Buffett

"The discipline of paying a dividend gives investors confidence in a company's financial health and stability." — David Dreman

"I'd rather own a high-quality business that can reinvest in itself, but dividends provide a tangible return that cannot be manipulated." — Warren Buffett

4.5 VALUE STOCKS

"A value stock is one that is underpriced by the market, but it still needs to have a solid foundation and growth potential." — Warren Buffett

"In value investing, you are looking for a margin of safety – a company that is worth more than the price it is selling for." — Benjamin Graham

"Value investing is inherently contrarian because value stocks are typically those that others avoid." — Seth Klarman

"People tend to chase growth stocks and ignore value, which allows value investors to find good deals in the market." — Warren Buffett

"The beauty of value investing is that you get upside in your investment without needing to take significant downside risk." — Joel Greenblatt

"Buying value stocks requires patience because the market takes time to recognize the value of a company." — Mohnish Pabrai

"Patience and discipline are necessary when investing in value stocks, as they are often slow to rise in price." — Charlie Munger

"Investing in value stocks is like buying a house in a good neighborhood. You're in it for the long term and can trust that value will grow." — Peter Lynch

"The benefits of value investing are not obvious in the short term but can be very rewarding over the long term." — Bill Ackman

"Investing in undervalued companies allows you to buy a business for less than it's worth. This principle has served investors well over time." — Philip Fisher

"In buying value stocks, you are buying into businesses that have the potential for long-term gains, even if they lack immediate appeal." — Irving Kahn

"Price is what you pay; value is what you get." — Warren Buffett

"Buying a dollar for 50 cents is the essence of value investing." — Seth Klarman

"Value stocks give you some downside protection; they don't typically fall as much as the overall market in a downturn." — Christopher Browne

"Value stocks are not popular because they often appear boring or flawed. This is what gives value investors an opportunity." — Joel Greenblatt

4.6 INDEX FUNDS & ETFS

"An index fund is a portfolio of securities designed to mimic a market index." — Burton G. Malkiel

"An investor is not likely to obtain superior results by buying a broad cross-section of the market. The more diversification, the more performance is likely to be average, at best." — Lou Simpson

"If you cannot look inside yourself and know that you have a special gift, indexing the majority of your assets makes the most sense." — John Rogers

"Investing is a funny business. It's really easy to be average. Just buy an index fund. It's really hard to be above average." — Howard Marks

"By periodically investing in an index fund, the know-nothing investor can actually outperform most investment professionals." — Warren Buffett

"A low-cost index fund is the most sensible equity investment for the great majority of investors." — Warren Buffett

"Don't look for the needle in the haystack. Just buy the haystack!" — John C. Bogle

"Most investors would be better off in an index fund." — Peter Lynch

"Indexing is a marvelous technique, I wasn't a true believer, but now I am." — Charles D. Ellis

"Over the long term, the superiority of indexing is a mathematical certainty." — Jack R. Meyer

"Most investors, both institutional and individual, will find that the best way to own common stocks is through an index fund." — Warren Buffett

PART 5: CAUTIONARY TALES

5.1 TIMING THE MARKET

"Time in the market beats timing the market." — Ken Fisher

"Far more money has been lost by investors preparing for corrections or trying to anticipate corrections than has been lost in corrections themselves." — Peter Lynch

"I have never known anyone who could consistently time the market. And in fact, I've never known anyone who knows anyone who could consistently time the market." — Jack Bogle

"More money has been lost trying to anticipate and protect from corrections than actually in them." — Peter Lynch

"The idea that you can predict what's going to happen contradicts my way of looking at the market." — George Soros

"Trying to time the market is a fool's game." - John Templeton

"Market timing is a wicked idea. Don't try it. Instead, buy and hold." — Charles D. Ellis

"Do not attempt to time the market. If you are not in the market on the right days, your long-term returns will be diminished." — Christopher Davis

"The real key to making money in stocks is not to get scared out of them." — Peter Lynch

"I don't know anyone who has done it successfully and consistently. I don't even know anyone who knows anyone who has." —Jack Bogle, referring to market timing.

"Timing the market is a fool's game, whereas time in the market is your greatest natural advantage." — Nick Murray

5.2 SPECULATION

“Speculation is a loser's game. Because of the costs, it has to be a loser's game.” —John Bogle

“The typical experience of the speculator is one of temporary profit and ultimate loss.” — Benjamin Graham

"The individual investor should act consistently as an investor and not as a speculator." — Benjamin Graham

"Investments throw off cash flow for the benefit of owners, speculations do not. The return to the owners of speculations depends exclusively on the vagaries of the resale market.” —Seth Klarman

Speculation is most dangerous when it looks easiest — Warren Buffett

There are only two sources of return: enterprise (resulting from business profits) and speculation (resulting from the psychology of the markets) —John Maynard Keynes

"Investment is an activity of forecasting the yield on assets over the life of the asset; speculation is the activity of forecasting the psychology of the market."
—John Maynard Keynes

There is money to be made in those strange animals, options and futures. But, by and large, these are techniques for traders and speculators, not for investors. —John Templeton

"Speculation is an effort, probably unsuccessful, to turn a little money into a lot. Investment is an effort, which should be successful, to prevent a lot of money from becoming a little."
— Fred Schwed Jr.

"The investor's chief problem—and even his worst enemy—is likely to be himself. Speculation leads to more losses than gains."
— Benjamin Graham

"Speculators are obsessed with predicting, whereas investors are focused on price versus value."
— Seth Klarman

"The distinction between investment and speculation in common stocks has always been a useful one and its disappearance is a cause for concern."
— Benjamin Graham

"If you must speculate, do so with your eyes open, knowing that you will probably lose money in the end."
— Benjamin Graham

"The speculator's primary interest lies in anticipating and profiting from market fluctuations. The investor's primary interest lies in acquiring and holding suitable securities at suitable prices."
— Benjamin Graham

"Speculation is a dangerous game. It requires a degree of foresight that no mortal possesses." — Peter Lynch

"Speculation leads you the wrong way. It allows you to put your emotions first, whereas investment gets emotions out of the picture." —John C. Bogle

"In speculation, as in fishing, one sometimes catches fish but one always catches hell." — Edgar Lawrence Smith

5.3 COSTS AND FEES

"One of the astute things I was taught is that on average, the average investor does average before fees, and below average after fees." — Howard Marks

"Passive management does not give investors the return of the index; it gives them the return of the index less costs. So, the longer they have their money passively managed, the greater their underperformance will be relative to the index." — Bill Miller

"Beating the market averages, after paying substantial costs and fees, is an against-the-odds game; yet a few people can do it, particularly those who view it as a game full of craziness with an occasional mispriced something or other." — Charlie Munger

"I've often said that the efficient market hypothesis, or EMH, has a lot of truth to it, but the CMH — or "cost matters hypothesis" -- is eternally truthful to the last penny." — John Bogle

5.4 PAST STOCK PERFORMANCE

"It's stupid the way people extrapolate the past. And not slightly stupid, but massively stupid." — Charlie Munger

The past is never predictive. That something happened a certain way in the past doesn't mean it must happen that way in the future — Ken Fisher

"Don't think for a moment that small investors are the only ones guilty of too much attention to the rear-view mirror." — Warren Buffett

"There is a tendency to look to the past and say, these things have done well and therefore that's the way you should invest -- as opposed to saying where are the greatest investment opportunities going forward." — Bill Miller

"People are habitually guided by the rear-view mirror and, for the most part, by the vistas immediately behind them." — Warren Buffett

"If the stock market has a period of outperformance of its long-term return, it is inevitably followed by some period of underperformance. But people being optimistic and greedy by nature take the recent short-term outperformance of stocks as a sign of good things to come, rather than a warning of bad things to come." — Seth Klarman

"Many mistakes have been made in buying growth stocks on the theory that the future will duplicate the past." — Benjamin Graham

All anyone can buy in the stock market is the unknown future. The past is not for sale, someone has already had it. — Thomas Phelps

5.5 LEVERAGE AND DEBT

"The use of leverage is dangerous. It's like driving a car with a sharp dagger mounted on the steering wheel, pointed at your chest." — Charlie Munger

"Leverage is like adding dynamite to your portfolio. It may help you get rich quicker, but it can also blow you up." — Warren Buffett

"I've seen more people fail because of liquor and leverage — leverage being borrowed money. If you're smart, you don't need it; and if you're dumb, you shouldn't be using it." — Warren Buffett

“When you have a family, and a house, and the market is going down, and you're on margin, it's probably too much pressure for you to do the right research and the right kind of thinking to make good decisions.” — Peter Lynch

"Unquestionably, some people have become very rich through the use of borrowed money. However, that's also been a way to get very poor. When leverage works, it magnifies your gains. Your spouse thinks you're clever, and your neighbours get envious. But leverage is addictive. Once having profited from its wonders, very few people retreat to more conservative practices." — Warren Buffett

All borrowings increase the risk in a business — Thomas Phelps

"Leverage reduces a company's margin of safety. In tough times, high debt can push a company over the edge." — Bruce Greenwald

"In the world of investing, being comfortable with debt can be a slippery slope to financial ruin." - Mohnish Pabrai

"Leverage is a dangerous tool that can work against you as easily as it can for you." — Guy Spier

"Avoiding leverage may prevent you from getting rich quickly, but it will also prevent you from going broke quickly." — Benjamin Graham

"Using leverage to invest is like picking up nickels in front of a steamroller." — Warren Buffett

"A company with too much debt is like a powder keg; it might never explode, but if it does, the results are catastrophic." — Joel Greenblatt

"We don't like to depend on the kindness of strangers to meet tomorrow's obligations." — Warren Buffett

"Leverage is the only way a smart guy can go broke." — Charlie Munger

"High debt levels can cripple a company in tough times. Always check the balance sheet before investing." — David Dreman

"Leverage magnifies outcomes but doesn't change the underlying probabilities of success or failure." — Michael Mauboussin

"Using leverage is like playing with fire. It may warm you up, but it can also burn down your house." — Benjamin Graham

"Never invest in companies that require leverage to survive." — Warren Buffett

"Financial leverage is a knife that cuts both ways. It magnifies gains in good times and losses in bad times." — Howard Marks

"Avoid businesses with high leverage. Debt can turn a solid investment into a disaster." — Seth Klarman

Charlie and I always knew that we would become incredibly wealthy. But we were not in a hurry to get wealthy; we knew it would happen. Rick was just as smart as us, but he was in a hurry. And so actually what happened was that in the 1973-74 downturn, Rick was levered with margin loans. And the stock market went down almost 70% in those two years, and so he got margin calls, and he sold his Berkshire stock to me. I bought Rick's Berkshire stock at under $40 apiece, and so Rick was forced to sell shares at ... $40 apiece because he was levered. — Warren Buffett

Companies don't go bankrupt unless they have a lot of debt — Ken Fisher

5.6 UNDERSTANDING RISK

"The best investors do not target returns; they focus first on risk." — Seth Klarman

“Please do not forget that as the common stock level advances, the advantages of common stocks appear to be more attractive and the basic need for owning them becomes more persuasive in everybody’s reasoning. Yet in fact, common stocks undoubtedly become riskier as the price advances, and thus the risk increases as the widespread acceptance of common stock develops.” — Benjamin Graham

“If the stock market has a period of outperformance of its long-term return, it is inevitably followed by some period of underperformance. But people being optimistic and greedy by nature take the recent short-term outperformance of stocks as a sign of good things to come, rather than a warning of bad things to come.” — Seth Klarman

“It's important to recognize that the riskiness of investing comes only partly from the things you invest in. A lot of the risk comes from the behavior of the participants.” — Howard Marks

“Almost any asset can be risky or safe, depending on how other investors treat it.” — Howard Marks

“Risk is about how we make decisions, and only incidentally about the math that we employ to reach those decisions.” —

Peter Bernstein

“At its root, risk is about mystery. It focuses on the unknown, for there would be no such thing as risk if everything were known.” — Peter Bernstein

I am not willing to incur risk of substantial permanent capital loss in seeking to better long term performance.” — Warren Buffett

“Risk is how much can you lose and what are the chances of losing it.” — Seth Klarman

“You have to say to yourself, "If I'm right, how much am I going to make? If I'm wrong, how much am I going to lose?" That's the risk/reward ratio.” — Peter Lynch

“Real investment risk is measured not by the percent that a stock may decline in price in relation to the general market in a given period, but by the danger of a loss of quality and earning power through economic changes or deterioration in management.” — Benjamin Graham

"The more facts you can gather, the better informed you will be, and the less risk you will have." — Walter Schloss

"Risk comes from not knowing what you're doing." — Warren Buffett

5.7 LONG TERM PERSPECTIVE VS SHORT TERM PERSPECTIVE

Bear markets are emotionally trying and can make folks seek to reduce the near-term pain. That can mean making a radical change to investing strategy; one that may feel better now, but may not be appropriate long term. Ironically, it can end up hurting folks far worse than the pain they feel now... — Ken Fisher

I very frequently get the question: 'What's going to change in the next 10 years?' And that is a very interesting question; it's a very common one. I almost never get the question: 'What's not going to change in the next 10 years?' And I submit to you that that second question is actually the more important of the two -- because you can build a business strategy around the things that are stable in time. ... [I]n our retail business, we know that customers want low prices, and I know that's going to be true 10 years from now. They want fast delivery; they want vast selection. It's impossible to imagine a future 10 years from now where a customer comes up and says, 'Jeff I love Amazon; I just wish the prices were a little higher,' [or] 'I love Amazon; I just wish you'd deliver a little more slowly.' Impossible. And so the effort we put into those things, spinning those things up, we know the energy we put into it today will still be paying off dividends for our customers 10 years from now. When you have something that you know is true, even over the long term, you can afford to put a lot of energy into it. — Jeff Bezos

"Our favorite holding period is forever." — Warren Buffett

"Time is the friend of the wonderful company, the enemy of the mediocre." — Warren Buffett

"In the short run, the market is a voting machine but in the long run, it is a weighing machine." — Benjamin Graham

"Someone's sitting in the shade today because someone planted a tree a long time ago." — Warren Buffett

"The big money is not in the buying and selling, but in the waiting." — Charlie Munger

"The stock market is designed to transfer money from the active to the patient." — Warren Buffett

"All there is to investing is picking good stocks at good times and staying with them as long as they remain good companies." — Warren Buffett

"The best holding period is forever." — Warren Buffett

"Only buy something that you'd be perfectly happy to hold if the market shut down for ten years." — Warren Buffett

You need patience, discipline, and an agility to take losses and adversity without going crazy. - Charlie Munger

"The single greatest edge an investor can have is a long-term orientation." — Seth Klarman

5.8 USING MONEY MANAGERS, FUNDS OR INVESTMENT ADVISORS

"Money managers are not stupid. They realize that sticking one's neck out and producing short-term under performance that differs from an index that is used as the benchmark is risky." — Seth Klarman

"The mutual fund industry is not an investment management industry. It's a marketing industry." — David Swensen

"Worldly wisdom teaches that it is better for reputation to fail conventionally than to succeed unconventionally." — John Maynard Keynes

"Beating the market averages, after paying substantial costs and fees, is an against-the-odds game; yet a few people can do it, particularly those who view it as a game full of craziness with an occasional mispriced something or other." — Charlie Munger

"In my experience, large increases in assets under management adversely affect returns." — Seth Klarman

"I think it would be an interesting change for integrity if managers of funds were required to have more of their own money in them." — Seth Klarman

"If your preference is managed funds, you want a managed fund that, one might put it, is like a sailboat fighting not a typhoon of costs but only a breeze." — John Bogle

"On average, the average large-stock fund manager produces average returns before fees and below-average returns after fees. So compared with after-fee returns, an index fund is superior." — Howard Marks

"If all that can be promised is an average result, how can managers expect to be paid large fees for providing that average result?" — Benjamin Graham

"Beating the market averages, after paying substantial costs and fees, is an against-the-odds game; yet a few people can do it, particularly those who view it as a game full of craziness with an occasional mispriced something or other." — Charlie Munger

"If your preference is managed funds, you want a managed fund that, one might put it, is like a sailboat fighting not a typhoon of costs but only a breeze." — John Bogle

"If all that can be promised is an average result, how can managers expect to be paid large fees for providing that average result?" — Benjamin Graham

5.9 MOMENTUM INVESTING

"In the short run, the market is a voting machine, but in the long run, it is a weighing machine." — Benjamin Graham

"Momentum investing requires investors to assume something will continue simply because it is happening." — Howard Marks

"Investors are often their own worst enemies. Buying on the basis of short-term market momentum is one of the biggest mistakes they make." — Seth Klarman

“The tendency of investors to follow the market's momentum and bet on whatever has worked recently is accompanied by antipathy to whatever hasn't.” — Seth Klarman

“Fashions play their part in the stock market as in other affairs of life.” — Philip Carret

5.10 MARKET NOISE

"In the short run, the market is a voting machine but in the long run, it is a weighing machine." — Benjamin Graham

"Successful investing requires detachment from the noise of the markets. The best returns come to those who tune out the daily commentary." — Warren Buffett

"Most people get interested in stocks when everyone else is. The time to get interested is when no one else is. You can't buy what is popular and do well." — Warren Buffett

"Investing is about filtering out the noise and focusing on the fundamentals." — Howard Marks

"There are so many random elements in markets that it's easy to misinterpret noise as meaningful information." — Seth Klarman

"The less we pay attention to the news, the better our investments will likely perform." — Mohnish Pabrai

"Market predictions are mostly noise and guessing. The fundamentals are what truly matter." — Charlie Munger

"Most investors would do better if they had no idea what the stock market was doing." — Benjamin Graham

"Focus on the businesses, not the ticker symbols. Stock prices move around a lot in the short term and that's just noise."— Joel Greenblatt

"When others are fearful, the noise in the market becomes overwhelming. Those who succeed ignore it and stay focused." — John Templeton

"The trick is, when there is no clarity in the short term, not to let the noise mislead you from your long-term vision." — David Einhorn

"The intelligent investor is a realist who sells to optimists and buys from pessimists." — Benjamin Graham

"There's a lot of talk and noise, but not all of it is information. Knowing what's meaningful is the real skill in investing."— Howard Marks

"If you can stay cool while everyone else is panicking, you have a much better chance of seeing through the noise." — John Neff

"Most investors are obsessed with watching stock prices every day. But that's mostly noise. What matters is the long-term performance of the company." — Warren Buffett

"The single most important skill in investing is the ability to ignore short-term noise and focus on long-term value."— Philip Fisher

PART 6: VALUE INVESTING PRACTICE

6.1 WHERE TO FIND INVESTMENT IDEAS

"Invest in what you know." — Peter Lynch

"If you search worldwide, you will find more bargains and better bargains than by studying only one nation." — John Templeton

"I think I could make you 50% a year on $1 million. No, I know I could. I guarantee that." "You have to turn over a lot of rocks to find those little anomalies. You have to find the companies that are off the map – way off the map." I started at page one (of the Moody's manual) and went through every company that traded, from A to Z." —Warren Buffett

"Cloning is the fastest way to get good investment ideas." — Mohnish Pabrai

"You can find bargains among the stocks that are temporarily out of favor." — Joel Greenblatt

"The best investment ideas come from doing your own research, not from following the crowd." — Philip Fisher

"Invert, always invert: Turn a situation or problem upside down. Look at it backward — Charlie Munger

"Creating a checklist helps in identifying investment

opportunities by ensuring no important aspect is overlooked." — Guy Spier

"Unfashionable or neglected stocks often provide the best opportunities." — David Dreman

"Avoid following the crowd. Search out unpopular or unknown companies." — Sir John Templeton

"We look for dislocations and mispricings caused by temporary factors." — Seth Klarman

"Some of my best stock picks came from walking through malls and noticing what stores were crowded." — Peter Lynch

6.2 DOING THE RESEARCH

"Investing without research is like playing stud poker and never looking at the cards." — Peter Lynch

"If you don't understand the details of your position, you will eventually lose money." — Bill Ackman

"Do your own analysis. Don't trust it to someone else." —Michael Burry

"Before you invest in a stock, you should understand the company inside and out." — Peter Lynch

"The more facts you can gather, the better informed you will be, and the less risk you will have." - Walter Schloss

"Investors must recognize that they are responsible for doing their own research." — Seth Klarman

"The more you know about a company, the better your investment decisions will be." — Joel Greenblatt

"If you don't do your homework, you won't succeed." — Jim Rogers

"The single most important skill for being a good investor is doing your own work and being diligent." — Mohnish Pabrai

In investing, whoever turns over the most rocks wins — Gautam Baid

“I think I could make you 50% a year on $1 million. No, I know I could. I guarantee that.” “You have to turn over a lot of rocks to find those little anomalies. You have to find the companies that are off the map – way off the map.” I started at page one (of the Moody’s manual) and went through every company that traded, from A to Z.” — Warren Buffett

“You have to really understand the businesses that you’re buying through the medium of stocks. And unless you’re willing to put a lot into that, you shouldn’t expect to get much out of it.” — Warren Buffett

“Almost everybody on this planet has the brain power to make money in the stock market. The question is whether you have the stomach for it and whether you're willing to do a little bit of work? Those are the key elements.” — Peter Lynch

“The very existence of doubt creates the conditions for a big gain in the stock once the fears are put to rest. The trick is to put your fears to rest by doing the research and checking the facts -- before the competition does.” — Peter Lynch

"Investing without research is like playing stud poker and never looking at the cards." — Peter Lynch

"If you don't understand the details of your position, you will eventually lose money." — Bill Ackman

"Do your own analysis. Don't trust it to someone else." — Michael Burry

"Before you invest in a stock, you should understand the company inside and out." — Peter Lynch

"The more facts you can gather, the better informed you will be, and the less risk you will have." — Walter Schloss

"Investors must recognize that they are responsible for doing their own research." — Seth Klarman

"The more you know about a company, the better your investment decisions will be." — Joel Greenblatt

"If you don't do your homework, you won't succeed." — Jim Rogers

"The single most important skill for being a good investor is doing your own work and being diligent." — Mohnish Pabrai

"An investment operation is one which, upon thorough analysis, promises safety of principal and an adequate return." — Benjamin Graham

"Never invest in a business you cannot understand." — Warren Buffett

"Investing without research is like playing stud poker and never looking at the cards." — Peter Lynch

"Risk comes from not knowing what you're doing." — Warren Buffett

"The very existence of doubt creates the conditions for a big gain in the stock once the fears are put to rest. The trick is to put your fears to rest by doing the research and checking the facts -- before the competition does." — Peter Lynch

I feel that I'm not entitled to have an opinion unless I can state the arguments against my position better than the people who are against my position. I think I am qualified to speak only when I've reached that state. — Charlie Munger

They don't have to, but most folks lose money. They commit three common mistakes: They overpay, buy businesses they don't understand and neglect to take a long-term approach. These three fatal errors account for most stock market failure. — Ken Fisher

6.3 QUANTITATIVE VS QUALITATIVE ANALYSIS OF STOCKS

"You need both qualitative and quantitative factors to make a sound investment decision. Numbers tell the past; qualitative factors tell the future." — Philip Fisher

"Great investing requires a mix of quantitative rigor and qualitative understanding, knowing when to use each." — Mohnish Pabrai

"Quantitative aspects are crucial in value investing, but quality is the differentiator between a good business and a great one." - Charlie Munger

"The qualitative aspects of a business, like management quality and competitive advantage, can drive success beyond numbers alone." — Seth Klarman

"Without qualitative analysis, you're essentially driving blind. Numbers only tell part of the story." — Howard Marks

"Quantitative analysis gives us facts and numbers, but qualitative analysis tells us about people, product, and culture—equally important in investing." — Peter Lynch

"You have to get a feel for what's behind the numbers; they don't stand alone." — Warren Buffett

"Quantitative metrics help determine value, but qualitative insight gives us confidence in the long-term viability of that value." — Bill Ackman

"Analyzing management's integrity and competence is qualitative, but it's often more important than any number." — Joel Greenblatt

"You can find low valuations, but without qualitative factors like innovation or good management, a stock won't outperform." — Jean-Marie Eveillard

"Focusing purely on quantitative data without understanding the quality of the business is like reading half the story." — Christopher Browne

"Quantitative analysis reveals what the company has done, but qualitative analysis gives insight into what it might do." — Philip Fisher

"Valuing a stock isn't just about the numbers; you have to understand the business and the people behind it." — Walter Schloss

"Qualitative factors like brand, culture, and customer loyalty often determine the sustainability of financial numbers." — Warren Buffett

"Quantitative analysis gives us precision, but qualitative insight brings wisdom to investing decisions." — Seth Klarman

6.4 STOCK PICKING CRITERIA

Anyone wanting to make 100 to 1 in the stock market must focus on earning power (earnings yield) — Thomas Phelps

If you are looking for stocks that might one day sell at 100x your purchase price, the P/E ratio at the time you buy is highly important. If you can see a P/E ratio rising from 10 to 40, your stock's earnings need only rise 25x your starting level to give you $100 for your $1 investment — Thomas Phelps

The most profitable common stock investments come in the form of young, rapidly growing companies that are currently out of favor with Wall Street. — Ken Fisher

"Successful stocks don't have to be high-tech or fashionable. Look for companies that are selling at bargain prices." - John Neff

"Good management is critical; if you can't trust management, you shouldn't invest in the company." — Guy Spier

"The individual investor should act consistently as an investor and not as a speculator." - Benjamin Graham

"Investors should purchase stocks like they purchase groceries, not like they purchase perfume." — Benjamin Graham

"Understand the value of the business you're investing in and the price you're paying for that value." — Howard Marks

A hallmark of a great business is that it has consistently high ROE without the use of leverage — Monish Pabrai

"Invest in what you know." — Peter Lynch

"It's far better to buy a wonderful company at a fair price than a fair company at a wonderful price." — Warren Buffett

"An investment operation is one which, upon thorough analysis, promises safety of principal and an adequate return." — Benjamin Graham

"Buy companies with strong histories of profitability and with a dominant business franchise." — Warren Buffett

"Great investment opportunities come around when excellent companies are surrounded by unusual circumstances that cause the stock to be misappraised." — Warren Buffett

"If you are shopping for common stocks, choose them the way you would buy groceries, not the way you would buy perfume." — Benjamin Graham

"Know the difference between investing and speculating." — Benjamin Graham

If management owns substantial amounts of stock, they are the stockholder's partners. They have every incentive to make the shares become more valuable. They will be particularly protective of the company's balance sheet. — Ken Fisher

It is best if management's stock ownership is at least 10 times its combined annual salary — Ken Fisher

The difference between a good business and a bad business is that good businesses throw up one easy decision after another. Bad businesses throw up painful decisions time after time — Warren Buffett

6.5 USING A VALUE INVESTING CHECKLIST

No wise pilot, no matter how great his talent and experience, fails to use his checklist." — Charlie Munger

"The investment process must be defined, organized, and consistent. A checklist helps ensure you follow the rules and stay disciplined." — Warren Buffett

"Having a checklist before making an investment is crucial. It helps you to avoid obvious mistakes." — Mohnish Pabrai

"Investment success depends on the rigor of your process, and a checklist is the backbone of that process." — Charlie Munger

"A well-structured checklist improves your decision-making process and ensures consistency in how you evaluate investments." — Howard Marks

"Checklists are like guardrails — they prevent you from falling off the cliff of overconfidence and poor judgment." — Joel Greenblatt

"The key to avoiding mistakes is discipline. A checklist helps you stay on track when emotions try to sway you." — Peter Lynch

"Every great investor has a process, and a checklist is essential in keeping that process repeatable and objective." — Seth Klarman

"You must be able to answer every item on your checklist before you commit capital. It forces you to think deeply and critically."

— Ray Dalio

"In investing, it's what you don't do that often matters most. A checklist helps ensure you avoid the big mistakes." — John Templeton

"A checklist is your investment safety net, it ensures you don't overlook critical factors." — David Tepper

"Using a checklist forces you to be methodical and prevents you from rushing into decisions based on emotions." — Michael Burry

"An investment checklist isn't just a tool for beginners, even experienced investors benefit from following one." — George Soros

"No matter how confident you are, a checklist ensures you stay grounded and focused on the key factors that matter." — David Swensen

"A good investment checklist should challenge your assumptions and force you to consider risks you might otherwise ignore." — Howard Marks

"A checklist is essential for staying objective, especially when markets are volatile and emotions run high." — John Bogle

"Checklists are not just about finding opportunities but about avoiding pitfalls. They keep you rational in irrational markets." — Philip Fisher

6.6 DECISION MAKING

"The more decisions you make, the higher the chances are that you will make a poor decision." —Lou Simpson

"I believe the investor operates at a distinct advantage when he is aware of what path his thought process is following." — Warren Buffett

"In the stock market, you don't base your decisions on what the markets are doing, but on what you think is rational." — Warren Buffett

"A lot of great companies have made a lot of decisions you haven't heard about because they decided not to do something. Some of the best decisions they did do was to not do something." — Peter Lynch

"It's not the answers that make you good in this business, it's the questions you ask. If you ask the right questions you will always find out more than the next guy." — Michael Price

"One of the illusions that people on Wall Street have is that they can have perfect information on a stock." — Seth Klarman

6.7 EVALUATING COMPANY MANAGEMENT TEAMS

"Management teams that think and act like owners are the ones you want to invest in." — Charlie Munger

"When a great management team meets a lousy business, it's usually the reputation of the business that remains intact." — Warren Buffett

"I've seen companies with mediocre ideas succeed because they had great management. And I've seen great ideas fail because they had bad management." — Bill Ackman

"When evaluating a company, always remember: People are policy. The quality of the management team is as important as the quality of the business." — David Swensen

"In the long run, investing in companies with strong, ethical, and competent management teams is more important than the business model itself." — Howard Marks

"Management must have integrity and talent. If I don't trust them, I won't invest." — Warren Buffett

"The ability of management to execute on a vision is far more important than the vision itself." — Ray Dalio

"A good management team is essential for long-term profitability and shareholder value." — Benjamin Graham

"A great business with poor management is not a great

investment. It's the people who make the difference." — Carl Icahn

"The first rule of investing is to look at the management team. If they can't be trusted or they're not competent, nothing else matters." — George Soros

"I would much rather invest in a company with a B-level product and an A-level management team than the other way around." — Mohnish Pabrai

"Invest in businesses with competent management that has a clear and ethical approach to leadership. Integrity matters." — Seth Klarman

"Good management is about having a vision, executing it well, and treating shareholders with respect." — Philip Fisher

If management owns substantial amounts of stock, they are the stockholder's partners. They have every incentive to make the shares become more valuable. They will be particularly protective of the company's balance sheet. — Ken Fisher

It is best if management's stock ownership is at least 10 times its combined annual salary — Ken Fisher

"The quality of management is a key factor in determining whether a stock is a good investment, but it is also one of the hardest factors to evaluate." — Benjamin Graham

"A wise investor puts as much emphasis on management as on the numbers. Trustworthiness and competence are paramount." — Irving Kahn

"It is very difficult to identify companies that will be the long-term winners, but identifying great management teams with a clear strategic vision is one way to improve your odds." —

Howard Marks

"A great management team that owns a lot of stock in their own company is aligned with shareholders and incentivized to make sound decisions." — Joel Greenblatt

"Good management teams are candid and transparent. They should be straightforward about the business, whether it's doing well or facing challenges." — Mohnish Pabrai

"The integrity of management is crucial. If management can be trusted, it's easier to make long-term investments, knowing they will act in the best interest of shareholders." — Christopher Browne

"A great management team understands their business inside and out and knows how to invest its capital wisely for long-term growth." — David Einhorn

"In value investing, great management isn't just about operational excellence; it's about capital allocation. How management deploys free cash flow tells you whether they are focused on shareholder value." — Seth Klarman

"We are particularly concerned about the alignment between management and shareholders. It is essential that management shares the long-term vision of its shareholders." — Jean-Marie Eveillard

"If management owns substantial amounts of stock, they are the stockholder's partners. They have every incentive to make the shares become more valuable. They will be particularly protective of the company's balance sheet". — Ken Fisher

"An outstanding management team can often achieve more with fewer resources than a poor one can achieve with greater resources." — John Templeton

"We're looking for managements that are able and honest." — Charlie Munger

"When we own portions of outstanding businesses with outstanding managements, our favorite holding period is forever". —Warren Buffett

"Look for three things in a person: intelligence, energy, and integrity. If they don't have the last one, don't even bother with the first two." — Warren Buffett

"Go for a business that any idiot can run, because sooner or later, any idiot probably is going to be running it." — Peter Lynch

6.8 PORTFOLIO ALLOCATION / PORTFOLIO MANAGEMENT

"Asset allocation is the most important decision in investment management." — David Swensen

The goal of portfolio management is to maximize returns while minimizing risk." — Harry Markowitz

"The key to successful portfolio management is to have a deep understanding of risk and return." — Eugene Fama

You can only know so many companies. If you're managing 50 or 100 positions, the chances that you can add value are much, much lower." — Lou Simpson

"A primary determinant of which stocks become a core holding in the portfolio and receive a higher capital allocation are the predictability and reliability of the company's cash flows." — Alex Roepers

"Successful portfolio management is about asset allocation, not stock picking. Your mix of investments determines most of your return and risk." — David Swensen

"It's not enough to have a diversified portfolio; you need to understand how the components work together, particularly in times of market stress." — George Soros

"In investing, it's not about the market timing, it's about portfolio positioning for long-term success." — Howard Marks

"You only need to make a few good decisions in your investing lifetime, so concentrate your portfolio on the best ideas." — Mohnish Pabrai

"You have to adjust your portfolio when the facts change. Flexibility is key to managing risk." — David Tepper

"The most important thing you can have is a good strategic asset allocation mix, because that determines your risk and return more than anything else." — Ray Dalio

"Successful investing requires taking the proper asset allocation seriously. Your portfolio mix between stocks, bonds, and other investments is the most critical factor." — David Swensen

"Risk control is the most important element of portfolio management, and your asset allocation is the foundation of that control." — Howard Marks

"The most important decision in investing is the asset allocation decision, which should be based on long-term risk tolerance." — Jack Meyer

"Investors should look for ways to minimize risk in their portfolios through a carefully constructed asset allocation plan." — Bill Gross

"The single most important thing to do is ensure that you don't overexpose your portfolio to any one area of the market, and that means careful asset allocation." — Seth Klarman

"I believe that your asset allocation is the key to achieving your investment objectives, far more than picking the right individual investments." — Paul Tudor Jones

"Diversification is not just the allocation of assets among various industries or securities, but also geographically and in types of investments." — John Templeton

"Portfolio allocation is as much about limiting your downside risk as it is about increasing your upside potential." — Joel Greenblatt

"Your portfolio allocation should be designed for maximum return at minimum risk, but always aligned with your tolerance for volatility." — Ralph Wanger

"A concentrated portfolio is only suitable when you have high conviction in your ideas. If not, stick with a diversified allocation to reduce risk." — Mohnish Pabrai

"The holy grail of investing is to have 15 or more good, uncorrelated bets." — Ray Dalio

Reducing portfolio risk by investing in a wide range of unrelated assets is the "holy grail" for investors. A lot of people think that the way you make a lot of money is to come up with the best single, or few, bets. That's wrong. That approach to the game will knock you out. Investors should always remain humble and remember that "what you don't know is greater than what you do know. By diversifying into "10 or 15 good, uncorrelated investments," investors can reduce their risk by as much as 80% without sacrificing returns, risk reduction is really key" to building wealth. — Ray Dalio

6.9 PORTFOLIO DIVERSIFICATION VS FOCUS

Reducing portfolio risk by investing in a wide range of unrelated assets is the "holy grail" for investors. A lot of people think that the way you make a lot of money is to come up with the best single, or few, bets. That's wrong. That approach to the game will knock you out. Investors should always remain humble and remember that "what you don't know is greater than what you do know. By diversifying into "10 or 15 good, uncorrelated investments," investors can reduce their risk by as much as 80% without sacrificing returns, risk reduction is really key" to building wealth. — Ray Dalio

"We believe that a policy of portfolio concentration may well decrease risk if it raises, as it should, both the intensity with which an investor thinks about a business and the level of conviction he must have before making an investment." — Seth Klarman

"Diversification is protection against ignorance, but if you don't feel ignorant, the need for it goes down drastically." —Warren Buffett

"If you really know businesses, you probably shouldn't own more than six of them. If you can identify six wonderful businesses, that is all the diversification you need and you're going to make a lot of money." — Warren Buffett

"If you are not a professional investor, if your goal is not to manage money in such a way so you get a significantly better return than the world, then I believe in extreme diversification." — Warren Buffett

"Rather than own a little bit of everything, we have always tended to place our eggs in a few dozen baskets and watch them closely." — Seth Klarman

"I think the secret is if you have a lot of stocks, some will do mediocre, some will do okay, and if one or two of 'em go up big time, you produce a fabulous result." — Peter Lynch

"Diversification of risk matters not just defensively, but because it maximizes returns as well, because we expose ourselves to all of the opportunities that there may be out there." -—Peter Bernstein

"Diversification is a safety factor that is essential because we should be humble enough to admit we can be wrong." — John Templeton

"I view diversification not only as a survival strategy but as an aggressive strategy, because the next windfall might come from a surprising place." — Peter Bernstein

"The only time you're really diversified is when you have assets you don't want to own." — Peter Bernstein

"I think diversification and all the stuff they're teaching at business school today is probably the most misguided concept everywhere." — Stanley Druckenmiller

"There are huge advantages for an individual to get into a

position where you make a few great investments and just sit back. You're paying less to brokers. You're listening to less nonsense." — Charlie Munger

"Diversification is a damn poor surrogate for knowledge." — Marty Whitman

"Diversification is protection against ignorance, but if you don't feel ignorant, the need for it goes down drastically." -—Warren Buffett

"Maybe you're right 5 or 6 times out of 10. But if your winners go up 4- or 10- or 20-fold, it makes up for the ones where you lost 50%, 75%, or 100%." — Peter Lynch

"If you're lucky enough to have one golden egg in your portfolio, it may not matter if you have a couple of rotten ones in there with it." — Peter Lynch

"Diversification is protection against ignorance, but if you don't feel ignorant, the need for it goes down drastically." —Warren Buffett

"Our policy is to concentrate holdings. We try to invest significant amounts in a few companies that meet our criteria." — Warren Buffett

People who bet on all the horses at the race always have a winner but never make any money — Thomas Phelps

Reducing portfolio risk by investing in a wide range of unrelated assets is the "holy grail" for investors. A lot of people think that the way you make a lot of money is to come up with the best single, or few, bets. That's wrong. That approach to the game will knock you out. Investors should always remain humble and remember that "what you don't know is greater than what you do know. By diversifying into "10 or 15 good, uncorrelated investments," investors can reduce their risk by as much as 80% without sacrificing returns, risk reduction is really key" to building wealth. — Ray Dalio

No matter how careful you are, you can neither predict nor control the future. A hurricane or earthquake, a strike at a supplier, an unexpected technological advance by a competitor, or a government-ordered product recall—any one of these can cost a company millions of dollars. Then, too, what looked like such a well-managed company may turn out to have serious internal problems that weren't apparent when you bought the stock. —John Templeton

6.10 MONITORING YOUR PORTFOLIO / INVESTMENTS

"Investing without monitoring is like planting a garden and never watering it." — Peter Lynch

"Consistent monitoring of your portfolio is essential to manage risk effectively." — Ray Dalio

"You can't just set and forget your portfolio; markets change, companies evolve, and so should your investments." — Charlie Munger

"Reviewing your portfolio regularly allows you to ensure it still aligns with your financial goals." — John C. Bogle

"Frequent portfolio reviews help prevent small problems from turning into big losses." — Warren Buffett

"Monitoring your portfolio too frequently can lead to emotional decision-making." — Warren Buffett

"Investors should monitor their portfolios but avoid overreacting to market volatility." — Charles D. Ellis

"Review your investments at least annually to ensure they still meet your criteria." — Burton G. Malkiel

"Regularly review your portfolio to ensure that you're not over-concentrated in any one investment." — Peter Lynch

"Monitoring should be about making sure the fundamental reasons you bought a stock remain valid." — Joel Greenblatt

"Monitoring your portfolio should be about checking assumptions, not prices." — Howard Marks

"Regular monitoring can prevent small problems from becoming big ones." — David Swensen

"A well-structured portfolio requires periodic review to adapt to changing market conditions." — Ray Dalio

6.11 OUTPERFORMING THE MARKET

"With a casual attempt to beat the market, you're going to fail." — David Swensen

"The market doesn't know everything, but it doesn't know nothing, and knowledge is cumulative. The market knows stuff now that it didn't know forty years ago, so it's harder to outperform." — Howard Marks

"You can't outperform the market by doing the same thing the market does." — Howard Marks

"Outperforming the market is a matter of using reason over emotion, thinking independently, and maintaining discipline." — Seth Klarman

"The person who can sit patiently and stay rational when others are irrational will eventually outperform the market." — Peter Lynch

"The best chance of outperforming is having a contrarian mindset and being willing to go against the consensus." —

Mohnish Pabrai

"To succeed in the stock market, you must have the temperament to control the urges that get other people into trouble in investing." — Warren Buffett

"You have to be willing to be wrong and look foolish if you want to outperform the market." — Joel Greenblatt

"Outperforming the market means being selective, focusing on high-quality businesses, and ignoring short-term noise." — David Einhorn

"In the short term, the market is a voting machine, but in the long term, it is a weighing machine." — Benjamin Graham

"Patience, discipline, and a contrarian mindset are necessary to achieve returns greater than the market." — Bill Ackman

"The stock market rewards discipline, patience, and the ability to stay focused on intrinsic value." — Christopher Browne

"You have to be willing to invest in areas that others are avoiding or ignoring if you want to outperform." — John Neff

"If you follow the crowd, you will likely end up performing like the crowd. To outperform, you must go your own way." — Philip Fisher

"Outperformance comes from focusing on the long term and not getting caught up in the short-term fluctuations of the market."
— Jean-Marie Eveillard

"Over time, stock prices follow business performance. The key to outperforming is to focus on the businesses behind the stocks."
— Warren Buffett

PART 7: VALUE INVESTOR CHARACTERISTICS & BEHAVIORS

7.1 TEMPERAMENT OR EMOTIONAL FORTITUDE

"Most investors underestimate the stress of a high-risk portfolio on the way down." — Howard Marks

"Stoic detachment combined with emotional awareness is the perfect combination for stocks. Feel the fear, but let reason decide." — Joel Tillinghast

"In the stock market, the most important organ is the stomach. It's not the brain." — Peter Lynch

"Investing isn't about beating others at the game, it's about controlling yourself at your own game." — Arnold Van Den Berg

"For most investors in general, selling the expensive asset, and buying the cheap asset, seems like a logical strategy -- except when you actually try to do it. Because most people are actually not wired to be selling what's expensive and going up, and buying what's cheap and going down." — Bill Miller

"Almost everybody on this planet has the brain power to make money in the stock market. The question is whether you have the stomach for it and whether you're willing to do a little bit of work? Those are the key elements." — Peter Lynch

"If you're going to be in this game for the long pull, which is the way to do it, you better be able to handle a 50% decline without fussing too much about it." — Charlie Munger

"You need a temperament that neither derives great pleasure from being with the crowd or against the crowd because this is not a business where you take polls, it's a business where you think." — Warren Buffett

"When proper temperament joins with proper intellectual framework, then you get rational behavior." - Warren Buffett

"As soon as you realize you can afford to wait out any correction, the calamity also becomes an opportunity to pick up bargains." — Peter Lynch

"Everybody in the world is a long-term investor until the market goes down." — Peter Lynch

7.2 PATIENCE AND DISCIPLINE

"Patience is not simply the ability to wait—it's how we behave while we're waiting."
— Joyce Meyer

"The big money is not in the buying and selling ... but in the waiting." — Charlie Munger

"The stock market is a device for transferring money from the impatient to the patient." — Warren Buffett

"We don't have to be smarter than the rest; we have to be more disciplined than the rest." — Warren Buffett

"Being patient doesn't mean doing nothing. It means waiting for the right opportunities, not chasing momentum or hot stocks."
— Mohnish Pabrai

"The more you trade, the harder it is to add value because you're absorbing a lot of transaction costs, not to mention taxes." — Lou Simpson

"Consistency and patience are crucial. Most investors are their own worst enemies. Endurance enables compounding." — Seth Klarman

"Good investing requires a weird combination of patience and aggression. And not many people have it." — Charlie Munger

“The disadvantage of being in any kind of a market type environment - Wall Street would be the extreme - is that you get over-stimulated. You think you have to do something every day.” — Warren Buffett

“I don't want to spend my time trying to earn a lot of little profits. I want very, very big profits that I'm ready to wait for.” — Philip Fisher

“It is just appalling the nerve strain people put themselves under trying to buy something today and sell it tomorrow. It's a small-win proposition. If you are a truly long-range investor, of which I am practically a vanishing breed, the profits are so tremendously greater.” — Philip Fisher

“You can lose money very fast, in two months, but you very rarely make money very fast in the stock market. When I look back, my great stocks took a long time to work out.” — Peter Lynch

"Over many decades, our usual practice is to do nothing. Just because you have an ability to act doesn't mean you should." — Charlie Munger

7.3 FEAR

“There is a considerable tendency for common stock investors to do the greater part of their buying, both of "good" and "bad" securities, at high levels of the market. They are equally inclined to do the greater part of their selling at low levels of the market, a procedure which is not conducive to successful results.” — Benjamin Graham

“Most people sell stocks at low prices not because they have to but because they are scared.” — Benjamin Graham

“If you don't like to lose money and it affects your judgment, don't buy things that can go down a great deal.” — Walter Schloss

"The real key to making money in stocks is not to get scared out of them." — Peter Lynch

"By holding stocks for the long term, we can minimize trading costs and capital gains taxes." — Guy Spier

"A buy-and-hold strategy helps investors avoid the pitfalls of market timing and short-term trading." — David Dreman

"Our holding period can be forever, as long as we believe we are benefiting from the growth of intrinsic value." — Lou Simpson

"To be a value investor, you have to be willing [and able] to invest in stocks that are unpopular or unknown. You have to be able to look past the greed and fear that grips the market." —Joel Greenblatt

"Invest for the long haul. Don't get too greedy and don't get too scared." — Shelby M.C. Davis

7.4 GREED

"Be fearful when others are greedy and greedy when others are fearful." — Warren Buffett

"To be a value investor, you have to be willing [and able] to invest in stocks that are unpopular or unknown. You have to be able to look past the greed and fear that grips the market." -—Joel Greenblatt

“The chief hazard of a careful common stock program is not that it may bring unexpected losses, but that its profits will turn the investor into a speculator greedy for quicker and bigger gains - and therefore headed for ultimate disaster.” — Benjamin Graham

“Few decisions in life motivated by greed ever have happy outcomes.” — Peter Bernstein

“You lose money fast in the stock market. You can't make it fast.” — Peter Lynch

“You want to be greedy when others are fearful. You want to be fearful when others are greedy. It's that simple.” — Warren Buffett

"Greed can make investors blind to risks that are apparent to others." — David Einhorn

"Successful investing requires the ability to be patient and disciplined, not swayed by greed or fear." — Bill Ackman

"Investors should avoid the temptation of greed, which can lead to chasing overvalued stocks." — John Neff

"Avoiding greed and fear is essential in value investing; stick to your framework and be patient." — Mohnish Pabrai

"Greed and hope will cloud your judgments and lead to poor decisions." — David Dreman

"Everyone wants to make money in the stock market, but it's important not to let greed cloud your judgment." — Peter Lynch

Some investors are like Aesop's dog who lost the piece of meat in his mouth by biting at the bigger one reflected in the water — Thomas Phelps

"Invest for the long haul. Don't get too greedy and don't get too scared." — Shelby M.C. Davis

7.5 OVER CONFIDENCE AND HUMILITY

"Humility is an enormously important quality. You can't win without it. Survival in the end is where the winners are by definition, and survival begins with humility." — Peter Bernstein

"A lot of smart people think they're way smarter than they are, and therefore they do worse than dumb people. And it's very common to be utterly brilliant and think you're way the hell smarter than you are." — Charlie Munger

"Nothing so gives the illusion of intelligence as personal association with large sums of money." — John Kenneth Galbraith

"The single most important thing, if you want to avoid a lot of stupid errors, is knowing where you're competent and where you aren't. Knowing the edge of your own competency. And that's very hard to do because the human mind naturally tries to make you think you're way smarter than you are." — Charlie Munger

"People always want to believe that this time is different, that there's something new under the sun, and that through their own ingenuity they can wish away risk." — Seth Klarman

“It is not really within human nature to comprehend that you may not know everything you think you know, and, further, that what you believe in could change on a dime.”— Seth Klarman

“One of the things you learn in this business is humility because you see your mistakes the next day.” — Walter Schloss

“The times I have been most wrong are the times I thought I was most right.” — Peter Bernstein

“Speculators often prosper through ignorance.” — Benjamin Graham

“A large advance in the stock market is basically a sign for caution and not a reason for confidence.” — Benjamin Graham

“Gambling is a tax on ignorance. People often gamble because they think they can win, they're lucky, they have hunches, that sort of thing, whereas in fact, they're going to be remorselessly ground down over time.” — Edward Thorp

“We would rather underperform in a huge bull market than get clobbered in a really bad bear market.” — Seth Klarman

“Just because we think a stock is undervalued doesn't mean we're right. We may be wrong in our judgment.” — Walter Schloss

“I've thought a lot of things when I'm managing money with great, great conviction, and a lot of times I'm wrong. And when you're betting the ranch and the circumstances change, you have to change, and that's how I've always managed money.” — Stanley Druckenmiller

“Expertise is great, but it has a bad side effect. It tends to create an inability to accept new ideas.” — Dean Williams

“Nothing so gives the illusion of intelligence as personal association with large sums of money.” — John Kenneth Galbraith

“The single most important thing, if you want to avoid a lot of stupid errors, is knowing where you’re competent and where you aren’t. Knowing the edge of your own competency. And that’s very hard to do because the human mind naturally tries to make you think you’re way smarter than you are.” — Charlie Munger

“It is not really within human nature to comprehend that you may not know everything you think you know, and, further, that what you believe in could change on a dime.” — Seth Klarman

“It’s not given to human beings to have such talent that they can just know everything about everything all the time.” —Charlie Munger

“In the beginning of a stock market boom it is ever the "dear public," the fleecy lambs, the most guileless victims, who make the most money. They really do not know when to stop winning, and so in the end they lose profit and principal.” — Edwin Lefevre

If people are sufficiently persuaded of their own wizardry or that of others, they and their money will be separated.” — John Kenneth Galbraith

“I would rather sustain the penalties resulting from overconservatism than face the consequences of error, perhaps with permanent capital loss, resulting from the adoption of a "New Era" philosophy where trees really do grow to the sky." — Warren Buffett

"A lot of my stocks don't work. The beauty of the stock market is that if you are wrong, if you put $1,000 up, all you lose is $1,000. I have proven that many times." — Peter Lynch

"You must always be prepared for the unexpected, including sudden, sharp downward swings in markets and the economy. Whatever adverse scenario you can contemplate, reality can be far worse." — Seth Klarman

"The biggest investing errors come not from factors that are informational or analytical, but from those that are psychological." — Howard Marks

"The four most dangerous words in investing are: 'this time it's different.'" — Sir John Templeton

I feel that I'm not entitled to have an opinion unless I can state the arguments against my position better than the people who are against my position. I think I am qualified to speak only when I've reached that state. — Charlie Munger

"An investor who has all the answers doesn't even understand all the questions." — John Templeton

Some Scandinavian canoeists succeeded in getting through all the rapids of Scandinavia and they thought they would continue their success by tackling all the whirlpools in North America - the death rate was 100%. A big whirlpool is something you want to avoid. So is an intense ideology; particularly when your companions are all true believers. — Charlie Munger

7.6 FLEXIBILITY AND ADAPTABILITY

"I believe in maximum flexibility, so I reserve the right to change my position on any subject when the external environment relating to any topic changes too."
Henry Singleton

"When the facts change, I change my mind. What do you do, sir?" — John Maynard Keynes

"Contrarian investors must be adaptable to changing market conditions." — David Dreman

"Investing is a journey of continuous learning and adaptation." — Guy Spier

"Value investing requires a great deal of humility and flexibility." — Bruce Greenwald

"Investors need to be flexible to survive changing market conditions." — Seth Klarman

"You can't predict. You can prepare." — Howard Marks

7.7 BIAS AND SELF DELUSION

“The whole trick in life is to get so that your own brain doesn't mislead you.” — Charlie Munger

“We must remember that delusions swing between extremes, like pendulums. Delusions of grandeur and unending wealth give place to delusions of unending gloom. One is as unreal as the other.” — Bernard Baruch

“Difficult decisions require intellectual honesty, being able to see things as they are, not as you want them to be, and then facing up to problems and doing something about them.” — Arthur Rock

“Investors are right and wrong all the time for the wrong reasons.” — Howard Marks

“If I had to name one factor that dominates human bad decisions, it would be what I call denial.” — Charlie Munger

7.8 WORRY, STRESS, SELF- PITY

"With every company, there is something to worry about, but the question is, which worries are valid and which are not?" — Peter Lynch

"If you own stocks, there's always something to worry about. You can't get away from it." — Peter Lynch

"If you don't like to lose money and it affects your judgment, don't buy things that can go down a great deal." — Walter Schloss

"If you don't like to lose money and it affects your judgment, don't buy things that can go down a great deal." — Walter Schloss

Every time you find yourself drifting into self pity, whatever the cause, self pity is not going to help. Self pity can get pretty close to paranoia. You do not want to drift into self pity. Self pity is always counterproductive, it's the wrong way to think. And when you avoid it, you get a great advantage over almost everybody else - because self pity is almost always the standard response. And you can train yourself out of it. — Charlie Munger

7.9 SELF DOUBT

"For some reason, because of the way investor psychology works, people switch from only seeing the good to seeing only the bad." — Howard Marks

"The very existence of doubt creates the conditions for a big gain in the stock once the fears are put to rest. The trick is to put your fears to rest by doing the research and checking the facts - before the competition does." — Peter Lynch

"All investors need to learn how to be at peace with their decisions." — Seth Klarman

"Inflection points occur in the market, and around them performance can suffer, but you have to stick to your guns." — John Neff

"You have to know what you own, why you own it, and have conviction." — David Einhorn

"Too many investors over diversify because they are unsure of themselves. They lack the confidence to make decisions." —Peter Lynch

7.10 INDECISION

“Indecision has probably cost investors more than bad judgment.” — Arthur Zeikel

“Most investors tend to cling to the course to which they are currently committed, especially at turning points.” — Arthur Zeikel

"Indecision is the thief of opportunity." — Jim Rohn

"The investor's chief problem—and even his worst enemy—is likely to be himself." — Benjamin Graham

"If you wait for the robins, spring will be over." - Warren Buffett

"The inability to make a decision has often been passed off as patience." — Jim Rohn

"One of the biggest mistakes investors make is believing they have to do something." — Jim Rogers

“If the value of a company doesn’t just scream out at you, it’s too close.” — Charlie Munge

"The stock market is a no-called-strike game. You don't have to swing at everything—but when you see a fat pitch, swing for the fences." — Warren Buffett

"Too many investors over diversify because they are unsure of themselves. They lack the confidence to make decisions." —Peter Lynch

7.11 AVOIDING HERD MENTALITY

"You want always to think what not to do if you want to beat the index." — Charlie Munger

"There are two requirements for success in Wall Street. One, you have to think correctly; and secondly, you have to think independently."— Benjamin Graham

"I have a saying: "If everyone is going left, look right." Conventional wisdom is nothing to me but a reference point." — Sam Zell

"All of us, all of the time, have to be on guard against groupthink." — John Rogers

"Crowd enthusiasm, always greatest at the peak of a market, more often leads sensible men to behave foolishly. Nevertheless, the aim should be to have one's self well enough in hand to be immune to outbursts of mass emotion." — Fred C. Kelly

"Establishing and maintaining an unconventional investment profile requires acceptance of uncomfortably idiosyncratic portfolios which frequently appear downright imprudent in the eyes of conventional wisdom." — Howard Marks

"Herding is not necessarily something one does as the result of analysis. It is what one does when one's confidence is impaired." — Daniel Kahneman

"It is very hard to think against the crowd, especially when the crowd is practically universal and unanimous in thought and emotion." — Fred Schwed Jr

"Sometimes common sense tells us what statistics cannot." — John Bogle

"A public opinion poll is no substitute for thought." — Warren Buffett

"As history has taught us, most of the time, most of the crowd moves long after the optimum time to have moved is passed. So it is with investment trends, which start with the belief of a few and end with the conviction of the many." — Arthur Zeikel

7.12 MISTAKES, FAILURES, BIG LOSSES

"People who have had success in other parts of their lives have difficulty accepting how much failure there is in the stock market." — Joel Tillinghast

"I really believe it's better to learn from other people's mistakes as much as possible." — Warren Buffett

"I don't think it's productive to wallow in regret. But if you've lost money in a stock and you don't learn anything, that's wasted money. Figure out what it is that you did wrong and don't do it again." — Joel Tillinghast

"You know, we make mistakes. Some go from 12 to 10 and we sell them. Some go from 20 to nothing. In a 10-year period, you are going to have one or two that go from 20 to nothing. If you have more, it is bad." — Michael Price

"No method guarantees you're not going to lose your shirt. I've done that many times. I've had stocks go from $11 to seven cents." — Peter Lynch

"If you're going to invest in stocks for the long term, or real estate, of course, there are going to be periods when there's a lot of agony and other periods when there's a boom. I think you just have to learn to live through them." — Charlie Munger

Every time you find yourself drifting into self pity, whatever the cause, self pity is not going to help. Self pity can get pretty close to paranoia. You do not want to drift into self pity. Self pity is always counter productive, it's the wrong way to think. And when you avoid it, you get a great advantage over almost everybody else - because self pity is almost always the standard response. And you can train yourself out of it. — Charlie Munger

"Your success in investing will depend in part on your character and guts and in part on your ability to realize at the height of ebullience and the depth of despair alike that this too shall pass." — Jack Bogle

"The most important thing to do if you find yourself in a hole is to stop digging." — Warren Buffett

"I think it's part of a life lived right that you learn how to make some lemonade out of your lemons." — Charlie Munger

All investors make mistakes. Even the very best – repeatedly. I make mistakes – lots of them. Some huge ones! I'll make more in the future – I promise. If you think you won't, you're wrong. — Ken Fisher

7.12 DEALING WITH UNCERTAINTY

“The more things people worry about the better for an investor, because those worries are already instantiated in the overall market.” — Bill Miller

“You never can predict the economy. You can't predict the stock market.” — Peter Lynch

“What you really want to do in investments is figure out what’s important and knowable. If it's unimportant or unknowable, you forget about it.” — Warren Buffett

“It's not uncertainty as such that bothers us, but unknowledge.” — Peter Bernstein

"I put heavy weight on certainty. It's not risky to buy securities at a fraction of what they're worth." — Warren Buffett

"The paralysis of analysis causes paralysis." — Charlie Munger

"You have to be decisive. Indecision can be worse than wrong action." — Bill Gross

"Good investing is a peculiar balance between the conviction to follow your ideas and the flexibility to recognize when you have made a mistake." — Michael Steinhardt

"If you have waited for all the light to turn green before starting your journey, you will never leave home." — Warren Buffett

7.13 RATIONAL DECISION MAKING

"In investing, being rational means understanding what you don't know and refusing to be influenced by the crowd." — Sir John Templeton

"Investing without rational analysis is like gambling. The results will reflect the whims of chance rather than your own foresight." — Christopher Browne

"If you allow emotion to cloud your judgment, you will pay dearly for it. Rationality is the foundation of successful investing." — Irving Kahn

"Most investors end up losing because they lack rationality in volatile times; they react out of fear or greed rather than reason." — Jean-Marie Eveillard

"If you're rational, you won't overpay. If you're emotional, you'll pay any price. Rationality is a defense against overvaluation." — Seth Klarman

"The difference between good and bad investing is often a question of who remains rational under pressure." — Howard Marks

"Emotions are your enemy in the stock market. If you can keep your head when others are losing theirs, you have an advantage." — Warren Buffett

"Rationality in investing is not just desirable—it is mandatory. Emotional decisions lead to costly mistakes." – Mohnish Pabrai

"An investor needs to do very few things right as long as he or she avoids big mistakes. Rationality is crucial to avoid these mistakes." — Warren Buffett

"The difference between good and bad investing is often a question of who remains rational under pressure." — Howard Marks

"Emotional investing is like driving drunk. Rationality allows you to avoid taking risks that can destroy your financial health." — Phil Fisher

"Rationality requires discipline and patience. Without it, you will be at the mercy of market cycles and emotional impulses." — Bill Ackman

"The market can remain irrational longer than you can remain solvent. Rational decision-making means avoiding the urge to follow the crowd." — John Maynard Keynes

7.14 PSYCHOLOGY OF INVESTING

“People do not consciously choose to invest according to their emotions -- they simply cannot help it.” — Seth Klarman

“No matter how calm you are, no matter how long term an investor you are, no matter what your horizons, when the market is jumping around, you feel uncertainty in your gut and it's hard to resist that.” — Peter Bernstein

"We’re not generally enthused about businesses where we think the future economics will be way less than the current economics." — Charlie Munger

"I prefer simple businesses with low uncertainty, not cyclical ones where predicting the future is challenging." — Mohnish Pabrai

“Many mistakes have been made in buying growth stocks on the theory that the future will duplicate the past.” — Benjamin Graham

PART 8: MAKING TIME FOR CONTINUOUS LEARNING, THINKING, AND REFLECTION

8.1 MAKING TIME FOR THINKING AND REFLECTION

“We are sort of the polar opposites of a lot of investors. We do a lot of thinking and not a lot of acting. A lot of investors do a lot of acting, and not a lot of thinking.” — Lou Simpson

“We both insist on a lot of time being available almost every day to just sit and think. That is very uncommon in American business. We read and think.” — Charlie Munger

"An investor should act as though he had a lifetime decision card with just twenty punches on it." — Warren Buffett

"I just sit in my office and read all day." — Warren Buffett

"It's not brilliance or just about being smart. It's about being patient and thinking long and hard before making a decision." — Charlie Munger

"Successful investing professionals are disciplined and consistent and they think a great deal about what they do and how they do it." — Benjamin Graham

8.2 INVESTOR LEARNING & EDUCATION

"The most important lessons in investing are learned in the tough times." — Howard Marks

"I don't think it's productive to wallow in regret. But if you've lost money in a stock and you don't learn anything, that's wasted money. Figure out what it is that you did wrong and don't do it again." — Joel Tillinghast

"I'm a big fan of knowing the big ideas in pretty much all the disciplines -- the ones that are pretty easy to assimilate -- and then using those routinely in your judgments. That's just my system." — Charlie Munger

My attitude towards business school is that there are six courses which are critical and most of those are accounting." — Sam Zell

"I'm a big fan of knowing the big ideas in pretty much all the disciplines -- the ones that are pretty easy to assimilate -- and then using those routinely in your judgments. That's just my system." — Charlie Munger

"The only sound distinction in investment policies for one type of investor or another is based not on his financial position but on his financial competence and financial preparation." — Benjamin Graham

“No stock picker knows so much that he can't learn a trick or a tip from a peer.” — Peter Lynch

“I really believe it's better to learn from other people's mistakes as much as possible.” — Warren Buffett

"Don't reinvent the wheel. Look at what the great investors are doing and try to learn from them." — Mohnish Pabrai

“In my whole life, I have known no wise people ... who didn’t read all the time. ... You’d be amazed at how much Warren reads, at how much I read. My children laugh at me. They think I’m a book with a couple of legs sticking out.” — Charlie Munger

"I read 500 pages...every day. That’s how knowledge works. It builds up, like compound interest. All of you can do it, but I guarantee not many of you will do it". — Warren Buffett

PART 9: MARKET FUNCTIONING, MARKET CYCLES AND THE FUTURE

9.1 HEEDING THE LESSONS OF MARKET HISTORY

"In investing - any serious practitioner must make market history part of their continuing education, otherwise they're doomed to draw the same wrong conclusions time and again". - —Ken Fisher

"If all the world sees X and expects Y, but you know from testing history that Y doesn't happen all the frequently (or maybe ever) after X, you can bet against them and win - more often than not". — Ken Fisher

"A huge part of successful investing is just avoiding common errors most folks make repeatedly..." — Ken Fisher

"Bull markets are born on pessimism, grow on skepticism, mature on optimism, and die on euphoria." — Sir John Templeton

"One of the important factors behind the fluctuation between bull and bear markets, between booms and crashes and bubbles, is that investor memory has to fail us - and fail universally - in order for the extremes to be reached." — Howard Marks

"Knowledge of the past is indispensable to understanding and managing the future." — Arthur Zeikel

"The four most dangerous words in investing are: 'This time it's different.'"
— Sir John Templeton

"Markets can remain irrational longer than you can remain solvent."
— John Maynard Keynes

"There are two kinds of forecasters: those who don't know, and those who don't know they don't know."
— John Kenneth Galbraith

"Bubbles have happened before and will happen again. Knowing that should make us humble and cautious."
— Nassim Nicholas Taleb

"Financial history is a wonderful teacher. It tells us that the improbable and the implausible can happen."
— Jim Rogers

"Everything you need to know about market history can be summed up in one phrase: The market always goes up over time."
— Peter Lynch

"Investors repeatedly walk into the same investment traps, making the same mistakes as their predecessors."
— Seth Klarman

"History provides a crucial insight regarding market crises: they are inevitable, painful, and ultimately surmountable."
— Shelby M.C. Davis

"No matter how good your analysis and how sound your understanding of history – you will be wrong from time to time".
— Ken Fisher

"I have great love and respect for market history. As they say, those who don't study history are doomed to repeat it". — Ken Fisher

"If past history was all that is needed to play the game of money, the richest people would be librarians". — Warren Buffett

9.2 MARKET EFFICIENCY

"Market inefficiencies, like tax selling and window dressing, also create mindless selling, as can the deletion of a stock from an index. These causes of mispricing are deep-rooted in human behavior and market structure, unlikely to be extinguished anytime soon." — Seth Klarman

"Stock market efficiency is an elegant hypothesis that bears quite limited resemblance to the real world." — Seth Klarman

"I believe the market accurately reflects not the truth, which is what the efficient market hypothesis says, but it accurately and efficiently reflects everybody's opinion as to what's true." -— Howard Marks

"To establish the right price for a stock the market must have adequate information, but it by no means follows that if the market has this information it will thereupon establish the right price." — Benjamin Graham

"I deny emphatically that because the market has all the information it needs to establish a correct price the prices it actually registers are in fact correct." — Benjamin Graham

"There is evidence that the stock market is more efficient in processing information about what other investors are doing than it is in processing fundamental information about the underlying assets, which is why stock prices so often turn out with hindsight to have been crazy rather than rational."

— Peter Bernstein

"People have always made money by taking advantage of inefficient markets." — Sam Zell

"Inefficiency doesn't make it easier for all investors to beat the market." — John Bogle

"Market inefficiency is what makes value investing possible; it creates the opportunity to buy bargains." — Howard Marks

9.3 MARKET ANOMALIES OR MISPRICING OPPORTUNITIES

"Market anomalies occur because human psychology is predictable yet irrational, especially in times of market stress."- —Seth Klarman

"Markets are often wrong in the short term, creating mispricings for disciplined investors willing to take advantage of them." — Howard Marks

"Sometimes stocks are valued below their intrinsic worth, which presents the intelligent investor with opportunities for above-average gains." — Benjamin Graham

"In the short run, the market is a voting machine, but in the long run, it is a weighing machine." — Benjamin Graham

"Mispricings happen because of fear, greed, and human error. A disciplined investor can exploit them by focusing on intrinsic value." — David Einhorn

"Market inefficiencies can be identified by a diligent investor who is willing to search where others do not." — Joel Greenblatt

"Value investing is about identifying a company's true worth and buying it when it's mispriced by the market." — Christopher Browne

"People often make mistakes in the stock market because they react to emotions and short-term events rather than fundamentals." — Peter Lynch

"Contrarian opportunities arise from the herd mentality of investors, which often leads to significant mispricings." — John Neff

"Opportunities come infrequently. When it rains gold, put out the bucket, not the thimble." — Warren Buffett

9.4 BULL MARKETS / BOOM MARKETS / MANIAS / BUBBLES

"Bull markets are born on pessimism, grow on skepticism, mature on optimism, and die on euphoria." — Sir John Templeton

"There is a considerable tendency for common stock investors to do the greater part of their buying, both of "good" and "bad" securities, at high levels of the market. They are equally inclined to do the greater part of their selling at low levels of the market, a procedure which is not conducive to successful results." — Benjamin Graham

"Experience in former markets indicates that just as they are too high in bull markets, they get too low in bear markets." — Benjamin Graham

"We would rather underperform in a huge bull market than get clobbered in a really bad bear market." — Seth Klarman

"It's much more stressful to me when the market's soaring and everybody's excited, and everybody's talking about how much money they're making." — Bill Miller

"In the beginning of a stock market boom it is ever the "dear public," the fleecy lambs, the most guileless victims, who make the most money. They really do not know when to stop winning, and so in the end they lose profit and principal." — Edwin Lefevre

"It's in the nature of Wall Street to imagine that whenever a company sets a record for earnings, it will go on setting new ones." — Peter Lynch

"It is a safe prediction for me to make that, in future years as in the past, common stocks will advance too far and decline too far, and that investors, like speculators -- and institutions, like individuals -- will have their periods of enchantment and disenchantment with equities." — Benjamin Graham

"Bull markets and bear markets last long enough so that the average trader is likely to forget by the time the climax is approaching that any sort of movement is possible." — Philip Carret

"It's much more stressful to me when the market's soaring and everybody's excited, and everybody's talking about how much money they're making." — Bill Miller

"If the market's going wild and you want to be in it, you either have to lower your standards to stay in the game or you buy stuff which may not participate because it's not part of the game at that time." — Walter Schloss

"Once a boom is well started, it cannot be arrested. It can only be collapsed." — John Kenneth Galbraith

"Booms start with some tie-in to reality, some reason which justifies the increase in asset values, and then -- and this is the critical feature of speculative mood -- the market loses touch with reality." — John Kenneth Galbraith

"A large advance in the stock market is basically a sign for caution and not a reason for confidence." — Benjamin Graham

"We would rather underperform in a huge bull market than get clobbered in a really bad bear market." — Seth Klarman

"Every economic recovery since World War II has been preceded by a stock market rally. And these rallies often start when conditions are grim." — Peter Lynch

"Any contrarian knows that just as a grim present is usually precursor to a better future, a rosy present may be precursor to a bleaker tomorrow." — Seth Klarman

"We believe that if a market is so overvalued that you can only find a few stocks to buy, you are probably better off not buying anything." — Arnold Van Den Berg

"One of the biggest mistakes you can make is to think that overpriced and going down tomorrow are synonymous. Markets that are overpriced often keep going." — Howard Marks

"Every bubble has two components: an underlying trend that prevails in reality and a misconception relating to that trend." — George Soros

"It is a curious fact that although all booms are alike, all are different." — Edwin Lefevre

"One thing all of us know for sure is that the stock market doesn't go down just because a lot of folks think that it has entered the heart of looney land." — Robert Kirby

"What we do know is that speculative episodes never come gently to an end. The wise, though for most the improbable, course is to assume the worst." — John Kenneth Galbraith

"I didn't get rich by buying stocks at a high price-earnings multiple in the midst of crazy speculative booms, and I'm not going to change." — Charlie Munger

"The tour we've taken through the last century proves that market irrationality of an extreme kind periodically erupts -- and compellingly suggests that investors wanting to do well had better learn how to deal with the next outbreak." — Warren Buffett

The tree does not grow to the sky — Thomas Phelps

9.5 BEAR MARKETS, RECESSIONS, PANICS, CORRECTIONS, AND OTHER MARKET DOWNTURNS

You get recessions, you have stock market declines. If you don't understand that's going to happen, then you're not ready, you won't do well in the markets — Peter Lynch

"When I ran Magellan Fund, the market had 9 declines of 10 percent or more in those 13 years. I had a perfect record. All 9 times, my fund went down." — Peter Lynch

"Most investors underestimate the stress of a high-risk portfolio on the way down." — Howard Marks

"There will be bear markets about twice every 10 years and recessions about twice every 10 or 12 years but nobody has been able to predict them reliably. So the best thing to do is to buy when shares are thoroughly depressed and that means when other people are selling." —John Templeton

"It would be silly to expect every bear market to turn into the Great Depression. It would be equally wrong to expect that a fall from overvalued, to more fairly valued, couldn't badly overshoot on the downside." — Seth Klarman

“It is only in a bear market that the value investing discipline becomes especially important because value investing, virtually alone among strategies, gives you exposure to the upside with limited downside risk.” — Seth Klarman

“You get recessions, you have stock market declines. If you don't understand that's going to happen, then you're not ready. You won't do well in the markets. If you go to Minnesota in January, you should know it's gonna be cold. You don't panic when the thermometer falls below zero.” — Peter Lynch

“I've found that when the market's going down and you buy funds wisely, at some point in the future you will be happy.” — Peter Lynch

“Experience in former markets indicates that just as they are too high in bull markets, they get too low in bear markets.” — Benjamin Graham

“I've been fully invested at the start of all the major declines and I will be fully invested in the next one. I am not a market predictor, that's for darn sure.” — Peter Lynch

“We would rather underperform in a huge bull market than get clobbered in a really bad bear market.” —Seth Klarman

“If you’re going to be in this game for the long pull, which is the way to do it, you better be able to handle a 50% decline without fussing too much about it.” — Charlie Munger

“I don’t think it’s productive to wallow in regret. But if you’ve lost money in a stock and you don’t learn anything, that’s wasted money. Figure out what it is that you did wrong and don’t do it again.” — Joel Tillinghast

"After a stock market decline, people may perceive more risk than before when, in fact, the decline may have taken some of the risk out of the market." — Robert Shiller

"As a rule, Panics do not destroy capital; they merely reveal the extent to which it has been previously destroyed by its betrayal into hopelessly unproductive works." — John Stuart Mill

"I know that stocks represent fractional ownership in businesses and that, over time, the stock market will reflect their true intrinsic values. And crises bring worries and fears that make many investors forget that simple fact." — Francois Rochon

"Bull markets and bear markets last long enough so that the average trader is likely to forget by the time the climax is approaching that any sort of movement is possible." — Philip Carret

"A lot of people when they get negative on the market put 50% in cash, but unfortunately a lot of times when you get to that position it's just about when the market's about to rally."— Peter Lynch

"People who exit the stock market to avoid a decline are odds-on favorites to miss the next rally."
Peter Lynch

"Whenever you get a wild excess on the upside, the following correction doesn't just go back to normal; it almost always falls way below normal."
John Templeton

"We would rather underperform in a huge bull market than get clobbered in a really bad bear market."

Seth Klarman

“Any contrarian knows that just as a grim present is usually precursor to a better future, a rosy present may be precursor to a bleaker tomorrow.”
Seth Klarman

“A correction is a wonderful opportunity to buy your favorite companies at a bargain price.”
Peter Lynch

“Corrections are unpredictable. By selling stocks to avoid pain, you can miss the next gain.”
Peter Lynch

“Whenever you get a wild excess on the upside, the following correction doesn't just go back to normal; it almost always falls way below normal.”
John Templeton

“It's very understandable to have a quick, sizable correction, even if the fundamentals are fine.” — Peter Lynch

“So the stock market will definitely have a correction. Everybody will say that it is the end of the world. I predict it. They will say the big one's coming.” — Peter Lynch

It’s been an ideal period for investors: A climate of fear is their best friend. Those who invest only when commentators are upbeat end up paying a heavy price for meaningless reassurance.
— Warren Buffett

9.5 THE FUTURE

All investing consists of dealing with the future — Howard Marks

"All successful investing is based on foresight, but foresight alone is not enough" — Thomas Phelps

"Investors tend to project the past into the future, but the future is always uncertain. — Howard Marks

"I never try to predict the future. I try to prepare for it." — Ray Dalio

"The future will surprise you. The key is to be positioned in a way that gives you the flexibility to benefit from those surprises." — David Swensen

"Forecasts may tell you a great deal about the forecaster; they tell you nothing about the future." —Warren Buffett

"The future is inherently uncertain, and successful investing requires the discipline to stay the course when markets are volatile." — Jack Bogle

"What we do know about the future is that it will be different, and it will reward those who are patient and persistent in their approach to investing." — Charlie Munger

"You can't predict the future, but you can create the future by focusing on the long term." — Seth Klarman

"Markets always change, and the future is always unknown. Investing is about reacting wisely to those changes." — George Soros

"The greatest investors look beyond the noise of the present and plan for a future they cannot predict." — Joel Greenblatt

"The stock market will fluctuate, and the economy will have cycles, but a disciplined investor can thrive through it all by planning for the future." — John Templeton

"The future is never clear, and you pay a very high price for a cheery consensus. Uncertainty is actually the friend of the buyer of long-term values." — Warren Buffett

"Successful investing is about being prepared for the future without trying to predict it too precisely." — Howard Marks

"Most investors make decisions based on what they think the future will be, rather than preparing for multiple possible futures." — Carl Icahn

“We have the same problem as everyone else: It’s very hard to predict the future.” — Charlie Munger

"No matter how careful you are, you can neither predict nor control the future. A hurricane or earthquake, a strike at a supplier, an unexpected technological advance by a competitor, or a government-ordered product recall—any one of these can cost a company millions of dollars. Then, too, what looked like such a well-managed company may turn out to have serious internal problems that weren’t apparent when you bought the stock". — John Templeton

"If you start from the premise that we are living in an uncertain world, then optionality is the only way to outperform the average over the long run." — Nassim Taleb

Made in the USA
Monee, IL
04 November 2026

67382849R00098